Apprais

## About the author

Clive Fletcher is Professor of Occupational Psychology at Goldsmiths' College, University of London. After completing his PhD, he worked for some years as a consultant psychologist in the UK Civil Service before taking up his first academic post. A Fellow of the British Psychological Society and a former chairman of its Occupational Psychology Section, Professor Fletcher has been involved in teaching and research in the field of managerial assessment and appraisal for over 20 years, and has published many books and articles in this area. He is a co-author of the IPM book on *Psychological Testing*, and of the IPM's research report on *Performance Management*. He is a member of a number of journal editorial boards, including that of *Personnel Management*. In his capacity as a director of FDA Assessment and Development Consultants, and as a Chartered Occupational Psychologist, Professor Fletcher advises a wide range of organisations in both public and private sectors on psychological assessment and performance management.

*1*

# Appraisal

## *Routes to improved performance*

**Clive Fletcher**

**Institute of Personnel Management**

First published in 1993
Reprinted 1994

Phototypeset by Action Typesetting, Gloucester
and printed in Great Britain by
Short Run Press Ltd. Exeter

*British Library Cataloguing in Publication Data*

Appraisal: Routes to Improved Performance
Fletcher, Clive
I. Title
658.3
ISBN 0-85292-514-X

INSTITUTE OF PERSONNEL MANAGEMENT
IPM House, Camp Road, Wimbledon, London SW19 4UX
Tel: 081-946-9100  Fax: 081-947-2570
Registered office as above. Registered Charity No. 215797
A company limited by guarantee. Registered in England No. 198002

# Contents

# Preface and Acknowledgements

Writing a book which is supposed to be both fairly short and essentially practical in nature is a bit like some appraisals – an exercise in conflicting objectives. There are so many practical aspects of appraisal, many of which have entire books devoted to them, that one of the chief difficulties is knowing where to draw the line in giving detailed guidance. I have tried to focus on those techniques where the personnel practitioner may be less knowledgeable. This means that the book occasionally illustrates some fairly complex methods, with supporting references for those readers who want to go into them in even more depth. Some basic examples of appraisal documentation and techniques, however, are given in the appendices. Another principle (or perhaps, belief) that I followed was that many people who use books of this kind do not actually read them through – they simply refer to the sections they need and which are of specific interest to them. With this in mind, I have taken the risk of sometimes repeating myself on occasion, making the same point on separate occasions so that it is not missed by a reader who is sampling the book on a selective basis.

Turning now to some acknowledgements. The IPM have hit on a good way of influencing their authors to deliver manuscripts on time. Opening personnel journals and finding advertisements displaying photographs of one's book – accompanied by invitations to place advance orders for it, specifying the date of publication – all while one is still actually *writing* it, is calculated to induce mild panic and keep the author hard at it. However, I would like to express my appreciation for the support given to me by Matthew Reisz at IPM publications – he is one of those very few examples I have ever encountered of a commissioning editor who makes a genuinely helpful contribution to the writing of a book. Lynne Spencer, wearing both her hats of experienced former HR manager-turned occupational psychologist, kindly read through the manuscript and made numerous valuable points that improved the final product. I should also like to acknowledge the information and help given to me by a large number of organisations who have, at various times, let me delve into their appraisal systems as a researcher or as a consultant. Without their openness, this book could not have been written. Finally, my thanks to my wife Linda for her patient support while I was glued to the word processor, and to my son Daniel for his countless but always welcome and entertaining interruptions.

# Chapter 1

## Appraisal today

This is intended to be a *practical* book on appraisal. Its aim is to help those personnel professionals, consultants and line managers who have the responsibility for setting up appraisal systems or revising existing ones. Since the survey data (Long, 1986; Bevan and Thompson in IPM, 1992) shows that the vast majority of organisations already have some kind of appraisal arrangements in place, most readers are probably seeking to build on previous appraisal work in their organisation. It would be nice to think that this new building will be on sound foundations rather than on the ruins of an appraisal system that has become discredited, but experience suggests that this is not always going to be the case. There are few more persistent topics of dissatisfaction in organisations than the appraisal scheme.

Indeed, appraisal has become an emotive word (McBeath, 1990). This is partly because it tends to be done rather poorly and partly because in recent years much of the public sector has had performance appraisal thrust on it as a matter of government policy. Perhaps as a result of this, many organisations have displayed considerable ingenuity in thinking up alternative titles for what is often much the same process: 'Development Interviews', 'Work Planning and Review' and the like. The drift of these changes has been to emphasise the more forward-looking aspects of appraisal, and to play down the retrospective assessment element. But it takes more than a change of name to shift people's perceptions, and staff still usually refer to it as 'the appraisal' irrespective of any new label it has been given.

No matter how hard it is to devise a satisfactory performance appraisal scheme, there is no real alternative to turn to. Appraisal will take place in an unstructured and perhaps highly subjective form wherever and whenever people work together. They will automatically form judgments about their own abilities and performance and that of their colleagues. To try to deny this is

1

foolish. Have you ever talked to employees who had no opinions about their bosses, their peers, their subordinates, or themselves? Organisations that try to avoid the issue by not having an appraisal scheme will simply end up having the same processes occurring without them being open to scrutiny or to control, with all the potential for bias and unfairness that this holds.

So, appraisal is here to stay. But the wider context in which it is set has changed. The advent of performance management, with its more strategic and holistic approach to organisational and individual performance, gives performance appraisal a central role in a more integrated and dynamic set of HR systems. Potentially, as is explained more fully in Chapter 5, this offers an opportunity for performance appraisal to achieve more than it could do alone in the past. It also brings with it some more problems, too. Performance-related pay (PRP) is often a part of performance management – though it is by no means essential to that approach – and has become more widespread in the UK over the last few years (Bevan and Thompson, 1991). Inevitably, PRP tends to have some links with appraisal, and both research and experience indicate that this can create many pitfalls in constructing an effective appraisal scheme.

Another major change has been appraisal's wider application. Within the public sector, appraisal has been used in the Civil Service since the early 1970s, but now it has been introduced into schools, universities, health authorities and local government. These widely differing organisations present a fresh challenge for appraisal to demonstrate its relevance to such diverse needs and groups. However, the increased range of application does not simply cover types of organisation. There has been a steady trend towards covering more staff levels, too. Where once it was the case that just middle and senior managerial groups were appraised, we now find that top management, scientific and professional staff, secretarial and clerical staff and operatives are often included, although the nature of their appraisal may be somewhat different. A consequence of the wider application of appraisal is that it now takes in staff from more varied cultural and ethnic backgrounds. Managing diversity is very much part of what appraisal is about – though there is precious little written about it in the appraisal literature.

Finally, in terms of changes, many organisations have undergone quite radical restructuring in the last few years. They have become more organic and less mechanistic, with fewer management levels and more flexible modes of operating. Managers have to build and manage teams that cross organisational boundaries and may exist only for the duration of the immediate task. They also have to deal with more information and take on a wider range of responsibilities (Cockerill, 1989). The kinds of staff they manage are changing, too, with more of them being knowledge workers. The role and perspective of the personnel practitioner have shifted with the new approaches to managing and structuring organisations. These developments have far-reaching implications for appraisal practice.

This, then, is the backdrop against which performance appraisal has to be viewed and planned. All of the changes outlined, and their impact on appraisal, will be dealt with in some detail in the pages that follow. Because of them, writing a practical book on performance appraisal is not as straightforward as it might sound. What is practical and appropriate in one organisation is quite impracticable and unsuitable in another, and even within the same organisation the requirements of the various groups and levels differ. We are seeing the demise of the monolithic appraisal system. Doubtless the idea of a universally applied, standard procedure that stays rigidly in place for years (perhaps kept there by the weight of its own paperwork) will lumber on in some quarters for a while yet, but its days are certainly numbered.

This book will present for consideration a series of key issues in developing and implementing appraisal, a description of some of the ways of dealing with them that have been taken by various organisations, and an evaluation of these approaches. However, the reader will not find in these pages copies of umpteen varieties of appraisal forms and documentation, though some examples do appear in the appendices. It is not a book that places great emphasis on this aspect of appraisal, chiefly because there is little reason to believe that the forms themselves are all that important. Such is the remit of performance appraisal that a book on it has to cover a very wide range of complex topics and techniques — job analysis, management competencies, assessment centres, and so on. Many of these merit a book in themselves, so wherever relevant the reader will be given references to more specialised texts. The evaluation of the varying approaches to appraisal looked at here will be based on organisational experience and on research findings. It would be less than honest to pretend that such an evaluation could be totally objective, any more than appraisal itself. The author's own views and preferences will be clear enough from time to time. Arising out of the material reviewed, some examples of good − and not so good − practice will be identified which will, hopefully, help practitioners build effective performance appraisal schemes suited to the needs of both their organisations and the people working in them.

## Chapter 2

# Deciding on the aims of appraisal

### The Organisational Perspective

The most fundamental question facing an organisation that is setting up appraisal is what the aim of the exercise is to be. Get this bit wrong, and you can bet that whatever else follows, the appraisal system will not run smoothly — if it runs at all. To be sure, it is not hard to think up a number of aims that appraisal may serve, but the main problem is setting up a realistic and achievable agenda. The reader might like, at this point, to pause and write down either the aims of the existing appraisal scheme in his or her organisation, or what the aims of the new scheme should be.

Let us look at some of the aims that appraisal is commonly supposed to meet. One of the most frequently cited purposes of appraisal is to enable some kind of assessment to be made of the appraisee. This may be against some pre-set objectives, or it may be in terms of ratings on job competencies, or the like. But assessment, whilst constituting a core element of appraisal, is not in itself one of its fundamental objectives — assessment done for its own sake is of little value. What it provides is a basis for several key aims of appraisal, especially:

- *Making reward decisions.* The notion is that if you are to engage in any kind of equitable distribution of rewards, be they pay, promotion or whatever, then some method of comparing people is necessary. If an assessment of performance is made annually, it can be used to direct rewards to those most deserving of them. The principle underlying this is the desire to treat staff in a fair manner.
- *Improving performance.* One of the basic principles of human learning is that to improve performance, people need to have some knowledge of the results they are already achieving. Making an assessment and conveying it should enable this

5

and help enhance performance. An accurate assessment of performance is also likely to bring to light training and development needs, and so improve performance through this, too.

- *Motivating staff.* There are three ways that appraisal seeks to motivate employees. Since the earliest appraisal schemes, it has been an article of faith that giving feedback, quite apart from assisting in task performance, is something that motivates people. And there is some justification for this, as employees in all types of organisation frequently express a desire for more feedback. The assessment made in appraisal provides the basis for such feedback, and thus contributes to motivation. Secondly, assessment increases motivation by facilitating the fair distribution of rewards. And thirdly, setting targets that improve on previous performance is a further motivating device.
- *Succession planning and identifying potential.* By identifying good and poor performers, the appraisal assessment can enable the organisation to focus succession planning and resources on the individuals who are most likely to respond positively and effectively to it.
- *Promoting manager–subordinate dialogue.* This is not always stated explicitly as one of the aims of appraisal. However, providing a formal occasion for the two parties to discuss performance is a way of encouraging more contact between them.
- *Formal assessment of unsatisfactory performance.* In its most negative (and fortunately most infrequent) garb, appraisal can be part of the process whereby unsatisfactory performance is documented and used in evidence in disciplinary or dismissal proceedings.

These are some of the purposes that, in theory at least, can be served through having an appraisal scheme that includes some element of assessment. On the face of it, they seem entirely justifiable. Unfortunately, although each one in itself is indeed reasonable, together, they most certainly are not. All the above points reflect things very much from the perspective of the organisation and its needs. If managers and subordinates had exactly the same needs, all would be fine. Alas, they do not. The result is that the various aims of appraisal are very difficult to reconcile with each other in real life.

## The Participants' Perspective

If performance appraisal is to be constructive and useful, there has to be something in it for the participants – both the appraisers and appraisees (Dulewicz and Fletcher, 1989). They, after all, are the people who have to make it work. What does the appraisal situation look like from their viewpoint?

Taking the appraisees first, they often do want feedback, are interested in improving performance, have training needs and do want to have a chance for constructive dialogue with their bosses. They also usually believe in fair distribution of rewards. Although this might sound like a perfect match with the organisation's needs, it is all conditional on:

- their perceiving the assessment as accurate and fair
- the quality of their existing relationship with the appraiser
- the impact of the assessment on their rewards and well-being.

The first of these is a condition that seldom appears to be met. Perhaps it is because of all the biases that can creep into judgments about others, or the imperfections of memory, or lack of contact between appraisers and the appraised, but there is a lot of evidence that appraisees do not readily accept the more unfavourable aspects of their assessment. Even when there is sound evidence of poor performance, there can be little willingness to accept it. Although some people are more objective about themselves than others, and some are more resilient and able to take criticism without feeling wounded, in general, the capacity to take negative feedback without experiencing any threat to self-esteem is fairly low. When people do face threats to their self-esteem, the most frequent reaction is mentally to rubbish the message and/or the source.

This is not to say that it is impossible to have any meaningful discussion of performance in the appraisal, but it does indicate that such discussion has to be handled with the greatest care and that it may lead to defensiveness rather than to increased motivation. The chances of defensiveness are increased greatly if pay or promotion are affected by the assessment. It takes a remarkably dispassionate, honest and self-denying individual to remain completely objective when faced with an assessment that may have adverse financial consequences. If, on top of all this, the existing relationship with the appraiser is not a good one, then it is extremely unlikely that the assessment will be seen as fair and acceptable. The main purpose of the appraisal, for the appraisee, becomes one of fighting a defensive action.

The appraisers' agenda for appraisal is also often far removed from what the organisation would like it to be. In an article in *Personnel Management*, George (1986) asked 'Why is it that managers frequently reject the suggestion that appraisal can help them manage better, and that it represents a worthwhile investment of their time?' The reasons are not hard to find.

As already suggested, the person appraised will not always agree with the appraiser's views, irrespective of the objectivity and accuracy of the latter. The appraisers are all too aware of this; in addition, the more insightful of them realise that assessing others is a tricky business, and that either they may lack the information and evidence necessary to make a fair judgment, or they may have biases that affect the way they interpret the information they do have. So they have ample reason to feel apprehensive about the situation and the likely reaction they may get from appraisees – particularly if they have had rather limited contact with them on a day-to-day basis. The appraisal interaction has to be seen for what it is in the eyes of most appraisers – one isolated event in the year. It might not be so tricky to deal with if the effects could be contained within that one event, but the truth for many managers is that any adverse reactions from the person appraised can make working relationships more problematic for a long while afterwards. Small wonder, then, that managers are prone to avoid carrying out appraisals if they can, and where they cannot, they tend to give overly favourable ratings. Even this tactic – being generous in the assessment – is not without problems, as it not surprisingly generates unrealistic expectations about future rewards on the part of the appraisee and so simply stores up trouble for a later date.

In the case of genuinely high-performing subordinates, one might expect the appraiser to be only too happy to sit down and have the pleasure of passing on their satisfaction. After all, the appraisee's reaction will be no cause for concern, apart from their reasonable expectation that the appraiser will be able to accompany the words with some tangible reward (which is not always possible). Unfortunately, it is not unknown for managers to be reluctant to identify high performers to the personnel department, because they fear that they will lose them through promotion or transfer. On top of all this, developing subordinates has seldom ranked high in organisations' priorities, or been something that is rewarded. Indeed, the evidence indicates quite the opposite − that managers who are good at staff development are less likely to make rapid career progress. The message is further reinforced in some organisations by the lack of central action in response to recommendations that come out of appraisals, and the lack of response to failure to carry out appraisals at all.

For all these reasons, the annual appraisal is, for many managers, a high-risk activity with little immediate positive outcome or reward. Organisations typically set up appraisal with a mix of short, medium and long-term objectives. But in present times, immediate results rather than uncertain longer-term benefits are what most managers are expected to produce. The research (Napier and Latham, 1986) shows that appraisers see little value in appraisals, irrespective of whether the general tone of the feedback is positive or negative. More often than not, their agenda for the appraisal is not the same as that formally laid down for it by the organisation.

## Setting Realistic Aims for Appraisal

If there is so much potential conflict between the different aims of appraisal, and if the participants frequently have differing objectives, what can we reasonably expect of the appraisal process? The answer is − quite a lot, though not perhaps as much as has traditionally been demanded. The failure to realise that appraisal cannot do all that has been asked of it, and that there has to be something in the process that will be seen to be of benefit to the participants, has probably been the root cause of the lack of success of so many appraisal systems.

The question becomes one of priorities: what are the essential purposes of the appraisal system, and how are they to be identified? The most common way of determining this is for the personnel director and/or the personnel department to dream the whole thing up themselves. Sometimes (and increasingly of late) top management take a direct interest, too. The likely outcome is an appraisal system that is all about the organisation's needs, with scant attention paid to the perspectives of the appraisers and appraisees. To avoid such an undesirable and, ultimately, unworkable result, it is necessary at the outset to involve representatives of managers and staff. Some examples of this and the mechanisms for it will be given in Chapter 4.

Wider participation in the design of appraisal does not automatically make the process easier. There will be differing needs and perceptions which have to be reconciled through negotiation. The end product should represent something for everyone − a not impossible objective if the parties accept from the start that this is a joint venture that must have everyone's commitment if it is to be successful and worthwhile. The most usual divide is between top management, who want a primarily assessment-driven appraisal (but which in theory fulfils all the other goals as well), and appraisers and appraisees, who want the appraisal to be primarily oriented towards development and motivation. This schism is not easily bridged.

Research and experience suggest that the best option is to define the function of appraisal in terms of development and motivation. There are several reasons for this:

- this is acceptable and welcome both to appraisees and most appraisers
- it represents what is generally the highest priority for the organisation − a strategy for improving performance
- the effectiveness of appraisal as a device for assessing individuals relative to their peers is rather doubtful.

Some of the rationale for this last point, on assessment, will be given in the next chapter. However, some organisations' needs or perceptions are such that they will focus appraisal more on the assessment function. This book will therefore try to provide guidance on setting up appraisal schemes of either complexion. This is necessary because the aims of appraisal crucially affect the nature and content of the appraisal scheme. If the aim is primarily one of assessment, with a view to making comparisons between people, then the appraisal is centred on common dimensions or aspects of performance that all staff within a particular group can reasonably be assessed on. For a more motivationally oriented scheme, there is no requirement for common dimension ratings or the like, and the emphasis instead is on improving skills and setting personal targets. The nature of the various approaches to appraisal will be described in detail in the next chapter, along with the strengths and weaknesses associated with them.

## Chapter 3

# The content of appraisal

Within the broad distinction of appraisal for assessment and comparison on the one hand, and appraisal for development and motivation on the other, lie a number of methods and techniques that form the content of appraisal in each case. The main ones are reviewed here.

## Appraising for Assessment and Comparison

### Appraisal of personality

This strikes a somewhat historical note, as you would be hard put to find any current UK appraisal schemes that focused overtly on personality attributes. In the 1950s, however, it was a different story, with many appraisal forms listing what were essentially personality traits. This gradually died out due to its extreme unpopularity with appraisers and appraisees, although Holdsworth (1991) mentions a British retailing organisation that included the assessment of 'moral courage' in its appraisal scheme as late as the early 1970s, and plenty of other examples persist in the USA (Williams, 1981).

Whilst appraising personality is not in vogue, it would be a mistake to think that it has gone away altogether. There are certainly remnants of it to be found in more ambiguous form. So, for example, 'drive' (or one of its synonyms) might well feature as one of the job-related attributes that an individual is assessed on. The idea, of course, is to try to keep away from direct comment on personality, as this is an area of great sensitivity and any criticism on these grounds is likely to elicit defensiveness and even outright hostility. Also, it is hard enough for people to deliberately change their personalities over a protracted period, let alone to do it more or less overnight at the instigation of the appraiser.

Does this move away from appraising personality mean that personality is now viewed as irrelevant to work performance? Far from it, as the very considerable and sustained growth in the use of personality questionnaires (Robertson and Makin, 1986; Shackleton and Newall, 1991; Mabey, 1992) indicates. It is perhaps not entirely by chance that the decline in personality-linked appraisal was followed by the rise in the popularity of such questionnaires. They are chiefly used in selection, promotion assessment and individual development (see Chapter 8), which clearly demonstrates that organisations *do* feel personality to be important in determining performance. It is just that they have found another, more indirect but possibly more objective, manner of bringing personality into the picture in making basic personnel decisions.

## Appraising job-related abilities

A sensible approach is to try to keep appraisal firmly locked on to the job and the abilities needed to perform it effectively. This represents a more detached, less personal way of discussing performance, and one which in theory is less likely to be threatening to the appraisees' self-esteem. It also tackles skills and abilities that should be amenable to training, development and improvement. However, as with appraisal focused on personality attributes, the basic intention is usually to compare the individual with other people at the same level and in similar work roles.

The first question that arises here is: what job-related abilities should be appraised? The aim is to identify those abilities that are central to good performance and can discriminate between staff with varying levels of performance. There are a number of ways of going about this. The least effective, and also (alas) the most widely used, is to get together a committee or working group, usually consisting of personnel representatives and top management, to decide what the most important abilities are. This is a largely unsystematic procedure, which tends to be heavily influenced by the seniority of the group members. The fact that what it produces does not rest on any observable and quantifiable data can have unfortunate legal consequences.

Fortunately, more appropriate job analysis techniques are available (see Pearn and Kandola, 1988, for a full discussion of the topic). These include diary methods, direct observation, questionnaires and interviews. A further method, called the Rep Grid, will be described later when we talk about competencies. All these yield relevant information, though not always of the same kind:

- As their name implies, diary methods require the job holder to keep an hour-by-hour record of their activities over a set period. This should provide a clear account of how time is spent on the job, and what it involves. It does, however, rely on the conscientious completion of the diary and on the decision of the job holder as to what to record.
- Direct observation of people doing the job in question can be very useful in getting a feel for the job, and has the virtue of providing an external and perhaps more objective view. However, it is often difficult to arrange, is time-consuming and the presence of an observer is sometimes a distorting factor (people may behave differently when they are being 'watched').
- Questionnaire methods of job analysis generally present the incumbent with a series of job components or elements that they tick or rate in terms of their relevance to the job. Two well-known examples of this approach are the Position Analysis Questionnaire and the SHL Work Profiling System, which are briefly described in Box 3.1. Questionnaire methods are very good at providing quantitative information on what the job entails.
- Interviews with the job holders are useful for throwing light on the more social and psychological aspects of the work, as well as giving a more all-round perspective when bosses, peers and even subordinates of the job holder are included in the interview process. A special variation on the interview method is known as the Critical Incidents interview (Flanagan, 1954; Warr and Bird, 1968). This is a fairly variable approach which typically involves the job incumbents and/or their bosses being asked to recall incidents when the job seemed to go particularly well – when they performed at a high level and felt satisfied with their efforts – and ones when it had gone much less well. Having thought of a group of such incidents, the respondents are asked to talk them through, describing what happened, the nature of the situation, what they had done, and the consequences. The

idea is that by collecting such information and analysing it (though little clear guidance is available on just how to do this), you can build up a picture of the important attributes that determine success and failure in the job.

---

**Box 3.1: Questionnaire methods of job analysis**

(a) The *Position Analysis Questionnaire* (PAQ) was developed principally by an American psychologist called McCormick, with his colleagues Jeanneret and Meacham. At the time of writing, it is marketed in the UK by Oxford Psychologists Press. The PAQ analyses job elements and relates them to the basic human behaviours involved, regardless of specific technological areas or functions. It consists of 187 items relating to job activities or the work environment. The job analyst interviews the incumbent and rates each of the job elements in terms of importance, frequency and so on. These elements cluster into six broad areas to give a picture of the job structure:

- Information Input: where and how does the individual get the necessary information?
- Mental Processes: what reasoning, planning, etc. activities are involved in doing the job?
- Work Output: what physical activities are performed and with what equipment?
- Relationships with Others: what does the job entail in terms of relating to other people?
- Job Context: what is the physical and social job context?
- Other Characteristics: any other activities or conditions that are relevant to performance.

The PAQ can be scored manually or by computer, and because it has been around for some time it is backed up by considerable research literature and a large database.

(b) The *Work Profiling System* (WPS) was developed by Saville & Holdsworth Ltd (SHL) and is relatively new compared to the PAQ. It is a computer-based, integrated job analysis system based on the kind of principles that underlie psychometric test construction. The job analysis information is collected through a questionnaire completed (manually or on a computer) by the incumbent. There are three such questionnaires, covering manual and technical, service and administrative, and managerial and professional roles. Respondents are required to:

- Write down their main job objectives
- Select a number of task categories (a set of tasks grouped together by function) which describe their job
- Rate the tasks (in the task categories) to indicate their importance for achieving their job objectives
- Rate the same items to indicate the proportion of time spent performing those tasks
- Rank the selected task categories according to their overall performance
- Provide responses to indicate the context in which the rated tasks are performed.

The data obtained are then analysed by computer. There are several outputs from this process apart from just a job analysis; it can, for example, produce person specifications and assessment method recommendations. The job analysis report focuses on tasks, context and the personal attributes necessary for the job. The WPS system is sophisticated and quite comprehensive, and allows for a wide range of use. As it is fairly new, it does not, as yet, have the research base of the PAQ, but early studies of its use show support for the method.

These approaches to job analysis will not necessarily always identify the abilities needed to do the job, but they will supply the information from which the latter can be inferred with a high degree of accuracy. Any one of them is likely to be superior to the so-called committee method. However, the best bet is often to combine two or more job analysis methods to gain a more comprehensive and accurate description of the job.

## Rating scales

Having identified the abilities necessary for effective performance in the job (though what follows applies also to the personality-based approach to appraisal), the next step is to form them into some kind of rating scales. There are numerous ways of presenting rating scales, and the main ones are illustrated in Box 3.2. Whichever one is chosen, a good deal of research suggests that people have difficulty in making meaningful distinctions if they are asked to handle more than seven categories. So rating scales should not have more than seven points. Some organisations feel that the advantage of having an even number is that there is no middle category, which thus forces the rater to make an assessment that points clearly to the upper or lower half of the scale.

---

**Box 3.2: Some rating scale formats**

Four types of rating scale format are presented here. The first two are far more widely used than the second two.

1 *Scales with verbally described intervals:* These can be illustrated by the following:

Overall performance

| Outstanding | Very good | Good | Fair | Not quite adequate | Unsatisfactory |
|---|---|---|---|---|---|
| ☐ | ☐ | ☐ | ☐ | ☐ | ☐ |

2 *Numerical (or alphabetical) ratings:* The individual is rated on a number of criteria using a scale ranging from best to worst, with a number or letter given to each interval point. For example:

Effectiveness with people

| | High | | | | Low |
|---|---|---|---|---|---|
| | 1 | 2 | 3 | 4 | 5 |

3 *Graphic rating scales:* These generally dispense with formal interval points apart from the two extremes and the middle, but define in some detail the behaviour associated with the quality being rated. For example:

Dependability is evidenced by the following behaviours (1) follows instructions (2) completes work on time (3) is punctual and regular in attendance (4) does not require excessive supervision.

HIGH ├───────────────┼───────────────┤ LOW

4 *Comparative scales:* The individual is rated on some quality in terms of his standing relative to others of his level. For example:

*Initiative*

A Not as good as the great majority
B OK, but many I have known have been better
C Typical of the middle group
D Better than most, though I have known better
E One of the best I have known

---

There are many advantages to using rating scales: they are easily understood; they offer a lot of flexibility; they encourage a more analytical view of performance by asking appraisers to think about the different aspects of the job; and of course they facilitate comparisons between people − which is usually their *raison d'être*. But there are also a number of problems and pitfalls associated with the use of rating scales, and it is worth outlining them here:

• Ratings are essentially subjective, which leads to a variety of distortions and biases creeping in. The most frequent one is the halo effect − one strongly positive attribute is allowed to colour the assessment of all the person's other attributes (see Box 6.1, Chapter 6 for a fuller outline of sources of bias). This leads to a lack of effective discrimination. Subjectivity can also leave its mark in the way scale titles are interpreted − for example, 'drive' means different things to different people.
• Appraisers are not very good at spreading their ratings across the full width of the scales. The most common findings are either a strong central tendency (nearly everyone is marked as average) or a positively skewed distribution (nearly everyone is rated highly). The reasons for this lie mainly in the problems appraisal poses for managers which were outlined in the last chapter.

The effect of these limitations is to undermine the fundamental purpose of having rating scales − to compare people. If assessments are subject to bias, if raters interpret the meaning of the same scales differently, if they fail to spread their assessments across the scale, then the appraisal does not provide the basis for fair and accurate discrimination between people of varying performance levels. Can anything be done to avoid these typical failings in the use of ratings?

Improving rating scales

There are four basic approaches to achieving more effective use of the rating method. They are:

• *Training.* Rating scales are, as already stated, easily understood − almost too easily. It is tempting to give impressionistic judgments without reviewing the evidence on which they are supposed to be based. The best defence against this is good training of appraisers at the outset. We will look at this subject in detail in Chapter 6.

- *Forced distributions.* If appraisers, when left to their own devices, do not distribute their ratings effectively, then they can be pressed by the personnel department to adhere to a set distribution. For example, 10 per cent get the top rating, 20 per cent the next to top, 40 per cent the middle, 20 per cent the one below the middle, and 10 per cent the lowest rating. In practice, the use of forced distributions is usually found in connection with overall ratings of performance, rather than on individual performance characteristics. It serves the purpose of making appraisers differentiate between appraisees, but at a cost. They may feel alienated by a system that so proscribes what they do. They and the appraisees may perceive some unfairness, and maybe justifiably, if some divisions have genuinely higher-performing staff yet have to apply the same distribution as lower-performing divisions. For these and other reasons, the use of rigid forced distributions is relatively uncommon now. However, many organisations do in effect manage to impose some control over the spread of assessment markings by more indirect means, as we will see when PRP is discussed later in the book (Chapter 4).

- *Increasing the number of raters.* If subjectivity is a problem, then one way of overcoming it is to involve more people in the rating process, on the principle that the combined judgments of several raters are likely to be nearer the truth than any one of them alone. The most frequently encountered versions of this are the combination of self-appraisal and superior-appraisal, and/or the use of more than one superior in the process (often the immediate boss and his or her own superior), but there are examples of schemes that have attempted to integrate superior, peer and self-appraisal (Stinson and Stokes, 1980); see Chapter 5 for a discussion of multiple source appraisal.

- *Behaviourally based rating scales.* This represents the most sophisticated approach to improving on the problems inherent in rating scale use. Essentially, it tries to put the appraiser into the role of an objective observer of behaviour rather than a judge, and seeks to minimise the scope for subjectivity. There are a number of variations on the theme:

- BARS: Behaviourally Anchored Rating Scales (Smith and Kendall, 1963)
- BES: Behavioural Expectation Scales (Zedeck and Baker, 1972)
- BOS: Behavioural Observation Scales (Dunnette, Campbell and Hellervik, 1968)

The first and third of these are the most frequently used examples, and they are explained and illustrated in Box 3.3 These methods are undoubtedly time-consuming to devise, which deters many organisations from using them, and various problems do arise. For example, managers are not always able to identify where on the scale they should place the behaviours they see; the anchors, after all, are only indicative, not comprehensive, behavioural descriptions. In addition, research evidence shows mixed results with BARS and their early promise of being technically superior has not always been borne out. However, because they are behaviourally specific, perhaps the value of these kinds of approach lies more in their potential to direct development than in their acting as superior assessment methods as such.

---

**Box 3.3: Behaviourally based rating scales**

The basic concept and methodology for all these approaches stems from BARS. The development of BARS goes through five stages:

- Examples of behaviours reflecting effective and ineffective job performance are obtained from people who are knowledgeable about the job to be rated.
- The examples are grouped into a series of separate performance dimensions by these experts.
- Another expert group repeats the second stage, allocating the examples to dimensions. They provide an independent check on the relevance of the behavioural examples to their dimensions. Any which are allocated differently by the two groups are probably too ambiguous and should be discarded. Also as a result of this, the dimensions should be quite independent of each other.
- Taking each dimension separately, the examples relating to it are rated by the experts in terms of effectiveness on a numerical scale. Where an example does not get rated similarly by different expert judges, then it will be deleted; a

high level of agreement on how an example is rated on that dimension is required.
- The resulting dimensions are each expressed as a scale, the points of which are anchored by the behavioural descriptions arrived at through the preceding stages. The number of dimensions can vary according to the job; anything from six to nine would be quite typical.

A variation on this method is offered by the use of BOS. Here, again, the end result is a series of performance dimensions linked to behavioural descriptions. The way the rating task is structured is rather different, though. Each behavioural example relating to the dimension is given a separate rating, and the overall dimension rating is the sum or average of these. Illustrations of BOS and BARS are given below.

### BOS example: teamwork dimension

TEAMWORK
(a) Tolerant to others and shows patience with them
Almost Always    1    2    3    4    5    Almost Never

(b) Consistently seeks to offer help and support
Almost Always    1    2    3    4    5    Almost Never

(c) Plays full and balanced role in team discussions
Almost Always    1    2    3    4    5    Almost Never

(d) Keeps colleagues informed where necessary
Almost Always    1    2    3    4    5    Almost Never

(e) Volunteers for fair share of less popular duties
Almost Always    1    2    3    4    5    Almost Never

(f) Willing to change own plans to cooperate with others
Almost Always    1    2    3    4    5    Almost Never

Here is the same kind of dimension, this time expressed in BARS format:

**BARS example: teamwork dimension**

50

Consistently seeks to
help others ————→

Tolerant and
supportive of
colleages ————→

Contributes ideas and
takes full part in group
40 ←———— meetings

←———— Listens to colleagues

Willing to change own
plans to fit in ———→
30

Keeps colleagues in
the picture about own
activities ————→

←———— Mixes willingly enough

Is not very aware of    20
what colleagues are
doing ————→

Inclined to alter
arrangements to suit
←———— self

Always criticising
←———— others
10

Lets everyone else do
the more unpopular
jobs ————→

Never goes out of way
to help or cooperate →

0

The use of training, multiple appraisers and BARS can lead to a
substantial improvement in the effectiveness of rating scales as a way
of assessing and comparing people. These refinements all take time

and resources to implement, but without them research and experience strongly suggest that the rating method will fail to discriminate fairly and accurately between people.

## Appraising to Motivate and Develop

### Results-oriented appraisal

The origin of results-oriented appraisal can be found in the Management-by-Objectives (MBO) movement that emerged in the 1950s (Macdonnell, 1989), although results-oriented appraisal is less systematic and comprehensive than MBO schemes tended to be. Essentially, the notion is that the appraisal session is one where manager and subordinate jointly review the latter's achievements against objectives or targets in the last six or twelve months, and then set objectives for the next period. As far as possible, the objectives are stated in quantified, time-limited terms, and in this they differ from aims, which are general statements of intent that are usually not specific in either timing or content.

One immediate effect of basing appraisal on results in this way is to shorten and simplify appraisal documentation. There is no need for rating scales and the like — the core of the appraisal form simply comprises sections describing performance against past objectives and the new objectives set for the year ahead. A set of headings for such a form can look like this:

| *Key* | *Priority* | *Action Needed:* | *Extent to Which* |
| *Objectives* | *Ranking* | *Who & When* | *Objectives Achieved* |

Under the last of these headings, the appraiser would record, at the end of the review period, the success the appraisee had attained. This approach to appraisal has steadily gathered popularity over the last 25 years, and is easily the most frequently encountered now. Why has it been so attractive?

The advantages of results-oriented appraisal are quite substantial, and chief amongst them is its greater objectivity. The whole point of quantifiable objectives is that it is easy to determine whether, or to what extent, they have been achieved. This means that there is a more reliable and valid measure of an individual's performance. This is obviously worth having in itself, but it has further and very significant knock-on effects. The greater objectivity serves to reduce some of the appraisees' concerns about the appraisal process, as well as the appraisers'. Perhaps partly because of this, results-oriented appraisal is a more effective motivating mechanism.

A large and consistent body of research findings (Locke *et al.*, 1981) confirm that setting targets is a powerful way of increasing motivation. Apart from its objectivity, this approach is supposed to be highly participative, giving the person appraised a much greater role and thus engendering a more positive attitude. When people commit themselves publicly to achieving goals they had some responsibility for defining, their self-esteem is bound up in the successful attainment of those goals.

In addition to its motivational qualities, result-oriented appraisal is by nature job-related, and therefore legally more defensible in terms of any personnel decisions taken as a result of it. It also involves some examination of the appraisees' priorities, which is a useful exercise that can avoid many misunderstandings that might otherwise arise. So, with all these advantages – objectivity, motivational power, participative nature, job-relatedness and so on – it is perhaps difficult to understand why results-oriented appraisal is not the only approach taken, let alone the dominant one. There are, however, some inherent limitations to going down this route.

The fundamental problem with appraisal centred on objective-setting is that it is difficult to make comparative assessments between people. Unless you have two or more people doing the same job in the same conditions and being set exactly the same objectives each year – circumstances that seldom, if ever, arise – then there is no common basis for comparison of the kind provided by rating scales. The reality of results-oriented appraisal is that differing goals will be set according to past achievements, present priorities and the appraisees' particular circumstances. If the objectives differ, it is difficult to compare the achievements of different individuals. It is not impossible to do so, but unless the comparison is in very general terms (exceeded target, attained target, fell short of target) and is made on the assumption that all targets are of equal difficulty (an assumption that will be discussed in a moment), a great deal of subjectivity will begin to enter the judgment.

The fact is that all targets are not, and should not be, equal in difficulty. They have to take account of the appraisees' capabilities. There is little point in pitching them so high that they are unlikely to be achieved, or making them so easy that they present no challenge. But then how do you compare the performance of these two hypothetical cases doing a similar job?

- *Appraisee A* has reached the quite modest performance targets asked of him. Although they are modest, they none the less represent a considerable achievement in view of his experience and abilities.
- *Appraisee B* has exceeded the objectives set. However, she has ample experience and ability, and the achievement has to be viewed in this context.

In other words, are we evaluating just the quantifiable attainment, or what that represents in terms of the individual's effort and ability? The answer is probably both, which is what makes results-oriented appraisal more difficult to use as a comparison mechanism. The picture is further complicated by the way appraisers and appraisees may collude to set objectives that make life easy for both of them – a little too easy for the appraisee to attain, so avoiding any need to discuss a short-fall in achievement.

There are some other drawbacks to results-oriented appraisal. One objection often raised is that not all jobs are amenable to framing in terms of objectives. There is an element of truth in this, though not as much as some would have you believe. I remember one senior university academic, who had presided over a faculty with a particularly abysmal research record, vehemently opposing the concept of objective-setting on the grounds that this was a nasty industrial concept of no relevance to academic work – how could you talk about enriching young minds in terms of objectives, etc., etc. It had to be pointed out to him that there were really rather a lot of relevant quantifiable objectives to consider, such as research output (e.g. number of articles published), course drop-out rates, and so on.

There is a point here, though. Whilst much – given a little thought and imagination – can be specified in terms of objectives, not *everything* that is important in a job is necessarily appropriately described in this way. There are dangers to evaluating performance exclusively in terms of ends rather than means. The examples of asking police officers to be assessed purely in terms of arrest rate, or surgeons to be assessed on numbers of operations should be enough to give pause for thought. The results attained are not, perhaps, enough to go on. External constraints also have to be considered: the individual's capacity to determine the targets achieved in the light of the resources available, the limitations imposed by circumstances, and so on. Any assessment has to take account of such factors. Partly because of this, the objectives set have to be reviewed at regular intervals to see if they are still appropriate or if they need modifying in the light of changes that have taken place.

So results-oriented appraisal is not as straightforward as it may first appear. It is certainly not an approach that lends itself to assessing and comparing people against a common standard. But it does have some very powerful arguments in its favour, not least of which is its potential for motivating individuals and improving performance − at least, in terms of end results. However, that is perhaps also its main limitation. As indicated earlier, there is a danger in over-emphasising ends at the expense of means. An example of this is provided by a business services organisation, where staff complained that managers were much more likely to be rewarded for achieving set financial targets than for being good at managing and developing staff. Not only does focusing exclusively on results direct attention away from the manner in which the results were achieved, but it may also leave a gap as regards developing individuals. It offers little in the way of a framework for analysing the skills and abilities the appraisee has acquired or needs to enhance. Mainly because of this, a number of organisations now try to combine the results-oriented approach with a competency-based appraisal system.

## Competency-based appraisal

The notion of 'competency' must stand a good chance of winning any competition for the most over-worked concept in HR management in the late 1980s/early 1990s. It is defined in a myriad of ways, which understandably leads to some confusion. Boyatzis (1982), whose work in the USA created much of the interest in this area, defines a competency as 'an underlying characteristic of a person', which could be 'a motive, trait, skill, aspect of one's self-image or social role, or a body of knowledge which he or she uses'. This is a very broad definition, and others adopt more succinct descriptions of what constitutes a competency, such as 'an observable skill or ability to complete a managerial task successfully' or 'behavioural dimensions that affect job performance' (Jacobs, 1989; Woodruffe, 1990) – either of which will suit the purpose of our current discussion.

There is actually very little, if anything, that differentiates competencies from the assessment dimensions used in many assessment centres for years. But competencies are applied more widely now, both by organisations and by bodies such as the Management Charter Initiative (MCI), in setting performance standards for managers. Some examples of competencies that have been used in major companies are given in Box 3.4. They illustrate the way in which the key competencies associated with high performance in an organisation can be incorporated into selection, training and development processes. Clearly, if they are being used in this manner, then they should have some place in appraisal. It makes sense for people to be appraised on the competencies that have been singled out as the most important for success.

Before looking at the operation of competency-based appraisal in more detail, the question of how to go about identifying the relevant competencies has to be addressed. This can be done by using most of the traditional job analysis techniques described earlier as a basis, but one method in particular has been used in many cases. This is known as the Rep Grid and was originally devised by a psychologist, George Kelly, as part of his Personal Construct theory of personality. Since then, it has been adapted to a wide range of other purposes, including a way of identifying – in behavioural terms – the broad dimensions or competencies that differentiate good from poor performance in a job or group of jobs. It is described in Box 3.5. Another method that has been used successfully is the generic competency questionnaire, which lists a wide range of competencies and their behavioural descriptions and asks respondents to rate each one in terms of its importance for effective performance in the company (Dulewicz and Herbert 1992).

**Box 3.4: Examples of competencies used in major UK companies**

(a) The first example is provided by Cadbury Schweppes (Glaze, 1989). They identify nine major dimensions of management competence:

- *Strategy*: vision, critical thinking, innovation, environmental awareness, business sense.
- *Drive*: self-motivation, initiative, tenacity, energy, independence, risk taking, resilience.
- *Relationships*: sociability, impact, acceptability, awareness.
- *Persuasion*: oral communication, written communication, flexibility, negotiation.
- *Leadership*: delegation, subordinates' development.
- *Followership*: followership, teamwork.
- *Analysis*: problem analysis, numerical analysis, listening, creativity, judgment, intuition.
- *Implementation*: planning and organising, decisiveness, organising sensitivity, management control, work standards, detail handling, compliance, stress tolerance, adaptability, commitment.
- *Personal factors*: integrity, management identification, career ambition, learning ability, professional/technical.

These are only partial descriptions of each competency. To show what a complete competency description looks like, the one for *Analysis* is given here; it breaks down into six components:

- Problem analysis: seeking pertinent data, recognising what is important, identifying possible causes, recommending action.
- Numerical analysis: Analysing, organising and presenting numerical data to support research and recommendations.
- Listening: drawing out information in face-to-face discussion.
- Creativity: introducing fresh ideas and insights, seeing new angles.
- Judgment: evaluating data and courses of action without bias or prejudice and reaching logical conclusions.
- Intuition: using hunch, feel and sixth sense to identify issues and possible solutions.

(b) In BP, (Greatrex and Phillips, 1989) the competencies fell into four groups:

- *Achievement orientation*: personal drive, organisational drive, impact, communication.
- *People orientation*: awareness of others, team management, persuasiveness.
- *Judgment*: analytical power, strategic thinking, commercial judgment.
- *Situational flexibility*: adaptive orientation.

Again, to go into a little more detail, two of the competencies are described more fully below:

**Personal drive** Self-confident and assertive drive to win, with decisiveness and resilience

| 1 | 2 | 3 | 4 | 5 |
|---|---|---|---|---|
| Decisive even under pressure, assertive and tough-minded in arguing his/her case, very self-confident, shrugs off setbacks | Will commit him/herself to definite opinions, determined to be heard, can come back strongly if attacked | May reserve judgment where uncertain, but stands firm on important points, aims for compromise, fairly resilient | Avoids taking rapid decisions, takes an impartial co-ordinator role rather than pushing own ideas | Doesn't pursue his/her points, goes along with the group, allows criticism or setbacks to deter him/her |

+ Indicators
- tough-minded driving style/pushes to get own way
- persistent in arguing points
- concerned to get solution he/she owns
- can confront others where important
- makes clear decisions when required
- commits self to definite opinions
- resilient to setbacks
- enjoys challenge, can accept mistakes
- maintains confidence

− Indicators
- rather soft or 'nice'
- doesn't pursue his/her points
- doesn't like confronting others
- inclined to give way if attacked
- lets others make the decisions
- backs off from giving definite view
- reacts emotionally to setbacks
- anxious, worried about mistakes
- lacking confidence, appears uncertain

**Team management** Ability to stimulate a productive team climate. Able to manage interaction of people with different perspectives, conflicting views

| 1 | 2 | 3 | 4 | 5 |
|---|---|---|---|---|
| Provides process leadership to promote team spirit and enthusiasm, builds others', commitment to achieve super-ordinate goals | Encourages others to contribute, will act as a facilitator for the group, builds alliances between people and groups | Balanced approach, will suggest methods and procedures for how to tackle the task | Tends to overstate the importance and value of one's own contribution, will reluctantly involve self in group | Prefers individualistic, self-centred approach, will tend to be indifferent to others and will do nothing about it |

+ **Indicators**
- uses humour to reduce tension
- tries to get agreement on principles
- behaves as a member of team and can get others to contribute
- draws out quieter members
- directs discussion by carefully-timed interventions
- encourages an open flow of communication between members
- process-oriented, facilitative

− **Indicators**
- attacks others, raises tension
- individualistic, not interested in group approach
- behaves unilaterally *eg* as the decision-maker
- ignores quieter members
- impulsive in his/her interventions
- becomes impatient with openness between members
- task-fascinated

It can be seen from these two company examples that although there are clear areas of overlap, the competencies also reflect idiosyncratic aspects of the individual organisations' needs and cultures.

### Box 3.5: The Rep Grid

The great advantage of the Rep Grid is that it allows the individuals interviewed to identify what they think is important in their own words; it does not force them into using some preconceived dimensions that the investigator has in mind. Taking its use in identifying competencies (so flexible is the technique that it can be applied to all sorts of other problems too), the steps in the process are given below. This is not the only way of doing it, though; there are many variations on the theme. The procedure is followed on a one-to-one basis with a manager one or two levels up from the job(s) being looked at, though job incumbents can also be included.

1. Ask the individual to think of six managers in the level or role under consideration. They need to be people the respondent has known well, who have worked in the organisation for two or three years, and who differ in effectiveness. Ideally, three would be above average or outstanding performers, while three would be below average or poor performers. The respondent does not have to name these people to the interviewer, but to facilitate remembering who they are the respondent is asked to write down some way of identifying each one of them (e.g. their initials) on a set of six cards. The better performers can be designated A, B, C and the other three as D, E and F.

2. The individual is asked to focus on cards/people A, C and E and to say — with their work behaviour in mind — which two seem more alike and different from the third. They are then asked to specify one aspect of work behaviour that reflects this. It is important that they (a) keep this to one aspect of behaviour, and (b) that their description has a verb in it — in other words, it is behavioural and not just a vague adjectival description. When they have done that, they also have to describe how the behaviour of the third person differs in this respect. The responses are recorded by the interviewer, who will ask follow up questions to probe the replies in order to refine and clarify the nature of the behaviour being described. In Rep Grid terminology, the dimension so elicited is called a Construct.

3. The procedure is repeated, this time with another triad — B, D and F. The same questions are posed, with the request that this should cover a different aspect of behaviour than for the first triad.

4. This is continued with further combinations of the six cases, making sure that none are repeated. It may be that the respondent will not be able to go through all the permutations without running out of new behavioural differentiations.

5. The interviewer may record the responses on a sheet as the session progresses, something like this:

| **Pair Alike**: A, E | **Single Different**: C |
|---|---|
| These two plan ahead; they take time to prepare in some detail | Always leaves things to the last minute. Does not think ahead; everything comes as a surprise to him |

The dimension here looks as if it centres on planning, but the exact nature of it does not matter too much at this stage, as the interviewer will want to administer the grid to several more respondents to get a good-sized and representative sample of views.

6. The grid can be analysed in a number of ways, and it is at this point that expertise and experience with the method is most needed. The simplest way is to label the dimensions that have come out in each respondent's grid, and then to go through them all, weeding out the ones that have not consistently been perceived as differentiating between high and low performers. Also, some of those dimensions that look a little different from one another (either within one person's grid or comparing across grids) will, on closer inspection, turn out to be the same thing in slightly different words.

Alternatively, and much more ambitiously, each triad differentiation can be put on a separate sheet of paper, and all of them mixed up so that they are no longer 'attached' to the respondent they were elicited from. Then the interviewer reads through all of them, sorting them into piles, each one of which is made up of replies that seem to reflect the same kind of dimension. When this is done, each group of statements is looked at again, and the precise nature of the dimension and the behaviours relating to it are defined.

From the above description, it will be appreciated that this method is far from quick. It can also run into problems in terms of managers not being able to think of enough cases of good and poor performers, or having such simple views on the world that they have only two or three constructs they use to differentiate people. But it does yield rich behavioural descriptions that, with further scrutiny, can form the basis of the competencies used by an organisation.

---

Whatever method is used to derive the competencies, one of the most important points to bear in mind is that the organisation cannot afford simply to observe the status quo. Framing the question in terms of what constitutes the main dimensions of effective performance now does not tell you what those dimensions will be in the future. Competencies are forward-looking, and should have within them elements that are anticipated as being the key attributes in five or ten years' time. Thus, some generic competency questionnaires ask respondents to rate competencies in terms of their importance now and, separately, five years ahead.

Having established what the key competencies are, they can be built into the appraisal system. Does this mean that they are to be part of what is essentially an *assessment* process, with people being rated and compared on their levels of competence? It is true that they could be used in this way, but that would rob them of much of their value. Competencies should not be equated with ratings of single job-related abilities. They are much broader and more complex than that. An individual may have mastered some aspects of a competency but not others. Ideally, the competencies used in appraisal would be represented in the kind of behavioural detail exemplified by the BP approach shown in Box 3.4. This allows for progression and development over time. Moreover, the competencies appraised might change as an individual's career progresses. It is unlikely that, say, a graduate entrant at the time of initial selection has had the opportunity to acquire and display all the skills and abilities that will be needed for success in an organisation. Some will only come after a fair amount of work experience. So while there will be some competencies that can be appraised from the outset, others will only come into the picture later.

Competency-based appraisal does allow some scope for comparing people, but its real strength is in analysing the progress of the individual and in directing attention to those areas where skills can be improved. It is developmentally oriented, and as such is likely to be motivating for the person appraised. The emphasis is on both parties in the appraisal working together to chart the levels of competence attained by the appraisee and decide the appropriate training and experience needed to make further progress. Because it is behaviourally based, it is more objective and less likely to generate disagreement or conflict − although it cannot be said that disagreements never occur. It does not deal with results achieved in any direct way, and is more concerned with the medium and longer term than with just the next 6−12 months.

## Overview of Appraisal Methods

The different approaches to appraisal that have been outlined in this chapter are not an exhaustive list, but they do cover those most frequently found. It will be evident that none of them are perfect.

All have their advantages and disadvantages, and achieve different things. The temptation for many organisations is to try and have their cake and eat it. They combine elements of the different approaches within the same scheme, in the hope that they will fulfil all the purposes they see for appraisal. The result is typically an appraisal scheme that has objective-setting alongside ratings of job-relevant behaviours and, probably, an overall rating of performance. Experience suggests that this is not a happy compromise, and that it does not overcome the contradictions and conflicts outlined in Chapter 2.

More constructively, an increasing number of organisations are putting together results-oriented appraisal with competency-based appraisal. This *is* a combination that can work well. It allows the more immediate and legitimate concern for achieving performance targets to co-exist with a focus on developing the appraisee – which in turn is related to the future performance of the organisation. It combines the two most motivational elements of appraisal, namely goal-setting and personal development. To maximise motivation and performance improvement, this would seem to be the most promising way forward.

## Chapter 4

# Appraisal as an element in performance management

The last ten years has seen the emergence of performance management as an approach not only to HR policies but to running the business as a whole. For many organisations, the term 'performance management' is synonymous with performance appraisal, or with performance-related pay (PRP). But performance management is much more than either or both of these. There is no single, universally accepted definition; indeed, it is perhaps better to think of it more as a philosophy than as a clearly-defined process or set of policies. The most prevalent notion of performance management is that of creating a shared vision of the purpose and aims of the organisation, helping each individual employee to understand and recognise their part in contributing to them, and thereby managing and enhancing the performance of both individuals and the organisation (Fletcher and Williams in IPM, 1992).

The main building blocks of such an approach are:

(1) the development of the organisation's mission statement and objectives
(2) associated with this, the development of a business plan (business being interpreted in the broadest sense of the word)
(3) enhancing communications within the organisation, so that employees are not only aware of the objectives and the business plan, but can contribute to their formulation
(4) clarifying individual responsibilities and accountabilities (which means, amongst other things, having job descriptions, clear role definitions, and so on, and being willing to be held accountable)
(5) defining and measuring individual performance (with the emphasis on being measured against one's own objectives rather than being compared with others)
(6) implementing appropriate reward strategies

(7) developing staff to further improve performance, and their career progression, in the future.

There are other elements to performance management that one could identify in various places — TQM is perhaps the most obvious — but these seem to be the main ones. From the above list it can be seen that performance appraisal and possibly (but not necessarily) PRP may be part of performance management, but integrated into a much broader approach.

However, there are some underlying principles that are not necessarily obvious from a simple list of elements of this sort, and which make performance management more than the sum of its parts. They are:

- Performance management is supposed to be owned and driven by line management, and not by the HR department or one or two directors — in marked contrast to many appraisal systems.
- There is an emphasis on shared corporate goals and values.
- Performance management is not a package solution, it is something that has to be developed specifically and individually for the particular organisation concerned.

You could add to these that performance management is something that applies to all staff, not just a part of the managerial group. This is certainly the case in some organisations, but by no means all.

If the performance management approach is successful, then it should result in more than just an improvement in the bottom line or the delivery of services:

- The culture of the organisation should be clearer and more readily identified with by those working in it.
- It should lead to higher levels of job satisfaction, job involvement and organisational commitment.
- It might be expected to have a positive impact on recruitment and retention, on quality issues, and on general human resources policy.

In fact, successful performance management is a holistic phenomenon and should have an impact on all aspects of the organisation's functioning. Not surprisingly, it has become the focus of an immense amount of interest and activity in both public and private sector organisations, ever-increasing numbers of which are developing performance management systems (PMS).

## How Appraisal Fits In

Performance appraisal has a central role to play in PMS. It is the usual vehicle by which the organisational goals and objectives are translated into individual objectives. It also remains the chief means of discussing and acting on the development of the individual. The difference is that, within the context of PMS, appraisal is now much more closely linked with the broader business context. This is illustrated in Box 4.1 by the case of a manufacturing company who operate an advanced PMS (see also Sheard, 1992). There are, though, a number of issues that arise or which gain greater prominence when appraisal operates within the framework of PMS. These are discussed below.

---

**Box 4.1 Performance management and appraisal: an example from a manufacturing company**

In this large, research-based organisation, the cycle starts with strategic company objectives being set by the board. These are then broken down and put into measurable terms for other management groups. They are discussed at team level and the members of the team may set their targets for the team as a whole. Individual managers have their role and job description agreed in the performance planning session, and agree their own targets in the light of the team targets. The importance of balancing team and individual achievement is highlighted in the appraisal training, as the company does not want to promote counter-productive competitiveness.

An individual's targets are reviewed when necessary, but at least quarterly, and on each occasion the person's development needs are also reviewed — with the emphasis on those with particular relevance to achieving the targets. There is an end-of-year review of success against those targets, which feeds into the reward system. Significantly, the single-sheet discussion record is held *only* by the person appraised, and there are *no* performance rating scales. The company has, however, invested considerable time and effort in identifying a set of key competencies that are used as a development tool. When development needs are agreed with the individual, it is up to the line manager to work with the individual to decide upon the appropriate means of meeting them — exemplifying the PMS approach of giving responsibility to the line rather than simply passing action on to the personnel department.

### Individual versus team achievement

One of the potential problems of creating a performance culture — which is what many organisations are seeking to do through adopting PMS — is that there is a risk of encouraging individual achievement at the expense of team effort and cohesion. This risk can be overstated, but it is important that when objectives are set in the appraisal, they reflect the priorities of the unit and not solely the narrower focus of the individual. This suggests that there has to be a clear understanding of the team goals, and that it would be helpful for some sort of group review and discussion to take place to facilitate this, before individual appraisals are carried out.

### Line-driven appraisal

The emphasis on line management driving PMS has implications for how appraisal operates. In terms of the purposes of appraisal, it accords with the views expressed in Chapter 2 on the importance of finding a formula for appraisal that meets the needs of the participants as well as the requirements of the organisation. It is essential that line management have a major input in determining the nature of the appraisal system; we will look at some detailed examples of this in Chapter 5. The line influence can go beyond simply saying what some of the aims of appraisal might be and extend to actually designing the forms and deciding on the way the system will operate. Part of the rationale for this is that line input will be sensitive to local needs and requirements, and will develop appraisal to suit these better than any centrally imposed scheme is likely to.

Whilst this level of line management involvement is laudable and welcome, and should raise commitment to the whole process of appraisal, it can create some problems. A company in the business services field found that when their line managers, as part of PMS, took on the design of appraisal schemes, the results were very mixed indeed. Different parts of the company adopted different approaches according to their needs. Some of these were sensible and worked well, but some were poorly designed and were ultimately failures. This hands-off approach by the HR department perhaps went too far. The example provided by a large local authority is probably a better model. Here, the HR department – after a consultative process – defined a core appraisal scheme, which the line management could add to and (up to a point) adapt to meet their departmental needs.

## Appraisal as part of a feedback loop

Another aspect of PMS that has an impact on the role of appraisal is the operation of a feedback loop. If PMS is to work effectively, it cannot be an exclusively top–down process. There has to be some mechanism whereby the strategic goals of the organisation and their implications at lower levels can be influenced and modified by the line. Without it, the chances of gaining commitment to the aims of the organisation are reduced. To some extent, this is covered by the emphasis on team discussion and the framing of team targets mentioned earlier. Such a mechanism necessitates an interim stage in the process, before individual targets are set in the appraisal, and should act as an opportunity to feed reactions to strategic objectives back to senior management. The appraisal itself also has some capacity to act as a feedback mechanism. Appraisees should be in a position to agree realistic and important targets rather than simply accepting those imposed on them.

The consequences of not allowing appraisal to operate in this way are illustrated by a major UK bank. Although PMS was set up through careful consultation and line management involvement, when it was implemented it was seen as a wholly top–down process. Managers complained that they were unable to negotiate their objectives, with the result that they felt little ownership of PMS and saw it as being driven by the HR department – despite the HR department having a fairly low-key facilitating role in the enterprise.

### Excessive bottom-line emphasis

The main thrust of PMS in many organisations is about bottom-line or service-delivery issues. This is understandable, but it can be taken too far. It brings back, in a slightly different form, the problem of excessive emphasis on ends rather than means. The concern becomes one of achieving short-term results at the expense of the longer-term aims – not least of which may be the development of the individual. Where it is part of PMS, appraisal may become so focused on the individual's targets and their achievement that the developmental aspect is neglected. If this happens, the appraisal process will fail to generate as much commitment from those appraised and will suffer in effectiveness. Worse still, excessive bottom-line emphasis in PMS can induce high stress levels that detract from employee well-being (Fletcher and Williams in IPM, 1992).

To some extent, the twin aims of achieving improved performance and developing individuals can go hand-in-hand, as illustrated earlier in Box 4.1. However, it may be the case that, in the context of PMS, holding development reviews separate from – but not unrelated to – the objective-setting and review process makes good sense. This kind of separation of appraisal functions into different occasions and sessions has long been advocated (Meyer, Kay and French, 1965; Randell, Packard and Slater, 1984), though more often driven by the need to take pay discussion out of the appraisal arena. With the emerging popularity of PMS, the merit of such an approach is increasingly evident.

## Appraisal and Pay

Performance management does not, of itself, have to embrace the concept of performance-related pay. However, PRP is more often than not a part of PMS, even in public sector organisations (Bevan and Thompson in IPM, 1992). The first thing to recognise is the importance of payment systems to organisations. The payroll takes up about 40 per cent of the total costs of the average manufacturing company, and in the case of public sector organisations this proportion can rise to around 75 – 80 per cent. Clearly, any changes to the basis for payment can have profound implications for the organisation as a whole. This is not a book about PRP, but it is so often linked to appraisal in people's minds and in practice, that it is crucial to devote some time to considering it in detail.

## Merit pay

There are lots of ways of relating performance to payment, but the one most frequently encountered in PMS is merit pay. This is where part (conceivably, all) of the basic salary increase is determined solely by the individual's performance. It is usually given annually, sometimes along with a cost of living rise, sometimes not. It generally falls within the range of 3 – 10 per cent of salary, though it can be more than this.

Survey findings repeatedly show support for the principle of merit pay amongst employees across a wide range of jobs and organisations. There is a strong and widely shared belief in the idea that those who perform well should gain greater benefits, and that allocating rewards this way is the fairest principle to follow. Thus, when a local authority offered staff the chance to transfer to PRP or to stay on the existing incremental system, they found that less than 3 per cent of the staff opted for the latter.

When we look a little deeper into this subject, however, we begin to see that the basis of the support for PRP is rather more questionable. It is neatly illustrated by a simple exercise carried out by an occupational psychologist (Meyer, 1980) who, some years back, asked all staff in a major company how they felt they were performing compared to their peers. He found that *on average*, people thought they were performing better than 75 per cent of their peers! And the higher you went in the company, the greater this proportion became. The implication of this is that people think PRP is fine chiefly because they assume that they are going to benefit from it. No doubt this is behind the example given by Wright (1991) of a financial services company where 75 per cent of the staff were in favour of PRP, but more than 70 per cent of them were rated as superior on their appraisals.

To some extent, then, the popularity of the idea of PRP may be based on widespread overly-positive self-appraisal, and an anticipation of the direct benefits PRP will bring to the individual. Consequently, there is a substantial problem of dealing with peoples' expectations when PRP is introduced – the majority are going to find they are getting less than they expected, and in some cases, a lot less. If money is to be attached to appraisal assessments, organisations cannot afford to go on permitting very positively skewed distributions of ratings, as it would have a serious impact on their financial viability. They have to make sure that the assessments follow a more normal distribution. Not surprisingly, a study (Pearce and Porter, 1986) of the impact of a new appraisal scheme showed that appraisees were unhappy at being assessed as average, and that they experienced a significant and stable drop in organisational commitment as a result. In my own research on performance management, I found staff who described getting the average assessment and pay award as a 'kick in the teeth'. Potentially, PRP has just as much power to de-motivate as to motivate.

There are other problems too. What do you do about employees who have performed well when the organisation as a whole has done very badly, and is in no position to award pay rises? How can adequate allowances be made for all the factors beyond the control of the individual in deciding whether their performance merits increased pay? And so on. The research evidence (Bevan and Thompson, 1991) does not show that adoption of PRP is associated with high levels of organisational performance. In itself, this is hardly surprising, any more than is the absence of a direct relationship between job satisfaction and performance. In both cases, one has to understand that performance on both the individual and the organisational level is determined by a multiplicity of factors.

It would be foolish to suggest that neither job satisfaction nor financial reward are important. But the simple-minded way in which pay is trotted out as the answer to motivating people at work flies in the face of all the evidence and theory. Certainly, financial reward can be a motivator for some people, some of the time. However, its effect is likely to vary hugely. Even within one person, the power of money as a motivator is likely to change radically depending on what life and career stage the individual is at. As long ago as the 1960s, research (Nealy, 1964) demonstrated that employees of different ages had very different reward preferences, and that the application of one incentive system to all employees in a particular job group did not make sense in motivational terms. We will return to this theme later.

By now it will be evident to the reader that there are many criticisms of the concept of merit pay and the way it tends to be used. None the less, it is often linked to appraisal in varying ways, and it is certainly not devoid of virtue, so it is important to examine the relationship in some detail.

## Direct and indirect links with merit pay

Performance appraisal systems that are geared primarily towards assessment for comparison purposes usually have the most direct link with pay decisions. Such appraisal systems typically use rating scales, and have an overall rating of performance that in some cases is the principal or only determinant of the PRP award. Here there is no ambiguity — a basic purpose of appraisal is to help establish an equitable basis for reward decisions. Employees who get the highest overall ratings are those who get the highest pay increases (or perhaps the only pay increases).

As we have noted earlier, in Chapter 2, the down-side of this approach tends to be its poor record as a motivating or performance improvement mechanism, which is rather ironic, given that one of the main reasons for adopting PRP is to drive performance. Because of the repeated problems experienced in tying appraisal too closely to pay, the majority of organisations have opted for a more distant link. Some of them still have overall ratings and are oriented towards making and conveying an assessment in the course of an appraisal. But they make the PRP decisions on a separate occasion and at a later date, allowing factors other than just the performance ratings to determine the outcome. This takes some of the heat out of the appraisal discussion, as no reward decision is immediately pending and the appraisee is not given the impression that the overall rating is the sole arbiter of what follows. However, the appraisal is still centred on reward-linked assessment, with some of the associated difficulties.

What happens when the appraisal scheme falls into the development and motivation category? Does this preclude having any links with pay and rewards? No, but the pay decisions are made on a different basis and usually by a different method. Instead of resting on an overall rating, they will relate to achievement against targets and/or increases in competence. And they are likely to be related to other broader factors, such as unit performance, individual circumstances and experience levels. In some organisations, the approach of getting groups of managers together to discuss intended PRP awards has been adopted. Such meetings, often presided over by a member of top management or by the HR department, have the purpose of ensuring that similar standards are being applied across the organisation, and that an individual manager's reward decisions are justifiable and accountable to peers.

There is clearly still a link between appraisal and reward in this approach, but it is a broader-based and less clear-cut one. It may be carried out at a different time to the appraisal — although difficulties can then arise over sequencing. It makes sense, in PMS, for the appraisal cycle to be tied-in with the business cycle. If strategic business goals are to be reflected at the level of team and individual target setting, then the latter have to follow the former in fairly short order. The review of achievement against targets logically takes place at or near the end of the next business year, and it is only at this point that the organisation knows what sums will be available (if any) for distribution in the form of PRP. This has the effect of bringing the pay decision back closer in time to the appraisal process, not in itself a very desirable thing. One of the ways around this evolved by some organisations is to have a separate development review (as opposed to the target review and setting session) a little while before the end of the cycle. This ensures that a constructive discussion can take place without the distraction of reward issues.

## Appraisal and wider reward policies

Besides merit pay, there is a whole host of financial inducements of varying kinds (Wright, 1991), as well as a potentially vast array of non-financial rewards. Promotion combines both, leading as it does to both more money and greater challenge and career opportunity (the question of appraising potential will be dealt with later, in Chapter 8).

Performance appraisal can live alongside some of these other reward strategies rather more easily than it can with merit pay. The use of one-off, unconsolidated bonus payments for exceptional performance, which might include such things as continuing to perform under especially difficult circumstances (e.g. short handed through staff illness) as well as achieving exceptional target performance, is becoming more popular. This does not cause too many problems for appraisal, as very few people qualify for such awards, and they are more likely to be widely recognised as deserving them since it is not simply a case of being above average, the category so many people like to identify themselves with. The fact that they do not lead to permanent pay differentials is another factor that makes them acceptable, whilst still being motivating to the individuals receiving them. Other financial rewards operating at a team or organisational level (such as profit sharing) also present less problems for appraisal. Because of their wider basis, they make less impact on the individual in the appraisal situation.

The use of non-financial rewards still seems to be very under-developed, though growing (Hilton, 1992). The point was made earlier that there are substantial individual differences in what motivates people, not only between individuals but within the same person at different life and career stages. Performance appraisal lends itself to the use of non-financial rewards that are tailored to the needs and preferences of the appraisee. Here are some examples of the kinds of reward that can be used:

- office decoration (prints, flowers, etc.)
- greater responsibility
- praise and positive feedback
- recognition from more senior/external sources
- greater exposure to more senior management
- enhanced job title
- conference attendance
- improved office and/or equipment
- assignments involving overseas travel
- sabbaticals.

Readers might like to pause a moment here and think of additions to this list that they would value themselves or could be applied in their organisations; there are many others that could be employed. Non-financial rewards do not, of course, automatically mean no-cost awards, but the first six items listed above, for example, have little or no expense attached to them.

Effective use of non-financial rewards in the appraisal process assumes two things. The first is that the scheme is set up to allow for it in the first place (though even if it is not, a manager with any initiative will still be able to get round this, up to a point). The second – and more difficult – is that the manager doing the appraisal knows what rewards to apply and when. This means possessing enough knowledge and understanding of the appraisee to be aware of what rewards that individual will appreciate at that time.

This is not commonly an element in appraisal training, but perhaps it should be. Nearly all appraisal schemes, even those that are essentially focused on assessment, purport to increase motivation, yet very few ever address this issue directly in training. Instead, they concentrate on the mechanics of the scheme and on the conduct of the appraisal interview. We will return to this subject when considering training in Chapter 6.

Giving non-financial rewards in appraisal does not usually generate the kind of problems associated with merit pay and some other forms of PRP. Perhaps this is because they are more individual and do not invite direct comparison, and because they often do not lead to permanent differentials. They are not valued the less for this, though. Many of them have the distinct advantage of being closer to intrinsic motivation than to extrinsic motivation. In other words, giving greater recognition, more responsibility, higher exposure to senior management and the like are all rewards that tap into the individual's pride in their work and achievement. Simply seeking to motivate with money sends the message that the reason for performing at a high level is personal financial reward. The question then arises: what happens to motivation and performance if (for various reasons, like economic recession) the money is not there any more?

## In Conclusion

Performance management sets some challenges for appraisal, but they are healthy ones. With its emphasis on greater involvement in and ownership of the objectives of the business, its focus on integrated effort in the development of a performance culture, and its concern with increasing motivation and development, performance management has the potential to make appraisal practices far more effective than they ever were when they operated more or less in a vacuum. Performance appraisal is the pivotal mechanism of a good PMS, and within such a framework it can − perhaps for the first time − achieve the high expectations that organisations have set for it.

# Chapter 5

# Designing appraisal systems

Many of the problems of appraisal systems arise out of the design process. Get it wrong here and it is likely to stay wrong. Design needs careful consideration of a number of issues. This chapter will go through them one by one, though in practice organisations seldom have that luxury – they have to be dealt with almost simultaneously and often rather quickly. But a little thought at this stage can save a lot of wasted time and effort later. Much of what has been said so far is a necessary precursor to this – not least the discussion of the aims of appraisal and where it fits in to the broader performance management picture.

## Aims (1): The Organisational Perspective

The very first step in designing an appraisal scheme is deciding its aims. Organisations who already have appraisal will have their reasons for changing their approach, and these will often determine what the aims of the appraisal will be. The mistake is usually to try to carry on with much the same aims and simply to adjust some of the administration and paperwork associated with it. If the scheme is to be reviewed, it is worth looking again at the purposes it is being put to. In today's fast-changing organisational environment, it is unlikely that any appraisal scheme will remain fully relevant to the needs and situation of the organisation for more than a few years; after that, it will need a thorough overhaul. This, apart from anything else, will keep appraisal in the front of people's minds and ensure that it does not lapse into becoming part of the bureaucratic history of the place.

The method of determining the aims of appraisal, whether reviewing an existing scheme or starting from scratch, has not tended to vary much. The usual device has been a working party dominated by the personnel department, with some top management input (the latter has increased in recent years). The agenda for appraisal therefore reflects their needs – collecting information for personnel decision-making and distributing rewards in many cases. Little attempt has been made to relate the appraisal process to the wider and longer-term needs of the business and the people driving it. To achieve the latter, a more strategically oriented approach is necessary. This might involve taking some very senior managers (including HR managers) away for a series of seminar-type events that encourage them to focus on the future direction of the organisation, and the implications for the kind of staff that will be needed and how they will be developed. Such events may take time and need some external facilitating agent, generally a consultant. Sometimes, quantitative information, from attitude surveys, Rep Grid exercises or other employee audit methods, is fed in to act as a basis for the discussion.

An increasing number of public and private sector organisations are using this kind of approach both to think through the problems already facing them and to anticipate those that they will face a few years hence. The aims and functioning of appraisal should be raised in this arena, and where they are considered, the resulting appraisal scheme is likely to look a lot more relevant and realistic in its intent than when it has just been the product of a working party set up for the purpose. None the less, these 'away-day' discussions can only provide part of the picture and should be just one element in a wider consultation process.

## Aims (2): The Consultation Process

We considered the perspectives of the different parties to appraisal in Chapter 2, and the point was made that ownership of the appraisal process is not something that should reside entirely with top management or the HR department − there has to be some kind of consultation process. The needs of top management, of the HR department, of the appraisers and the appraisees should all be reflected when determining the purpose and form of appraisal. While this means that the appraisal will seek to offer something to all involved, it also means that it is unlikely to give everyone everything they might want. In other words, the consultation process implies a degree of compromise in the pursuit of wider ownership of, and commitment to, the appraisal system. It requires negotiation of the aims of appraisal.

What does such a consultation process look like? There are

various approaches. One large retailing company got more than half their senior appraising managers to participate in group discussions in which they were presented with some initial proposals on a new appraisal system. These were subsequently modified as a result of the feedback given. A more comprehensive consultation process is described in Box 5.1 and this particular example illustrates another point about consultation. The author visited the organisation concerned in the early 1990s, by which time the company had changed hands and was − not surprisingly − rather different. The turnover in employees over such a long period meant that few of the staff had been there when the appraisal scheme had been devised. As a result, there was no longer a sense of ownership of the appraisal system − it was thought of as something that had come from the personnel department. This demonstrates one aspect of a general principle of appraisal, namely that any scheme has a limited 'shelf life'. Ownership only lasts as long as the participants and their memories of the consultation process; it needs to be revived in some form as part of the mechanism reviewing how appraisal is functioning.

As a result of the consideration of the aims of performance appraisal by the HR department and top management, and of the consultation with potential appraisers and appraisees, the general nature of the scheme − and maybe some of its specifics − will be set. These in turn will determine which of the various appraisal methods looked at in Chapters 2 and 3 will be required. Precisely how these are put into action, though, depends on other factors, described in the following sections.

## Organisational Structure and Culture

The structure and the culture of an organisation are dynamically interrelated, and both need to be considered in drawing up plans for an appraisal scheme. Is the company a highly structured, bureaucratic one where there is a lot of emphasis placed on formal observance of rules and procedures, and where power is vested in individuals largely as a result of their position in the hierarchy? If so, then the appraisal scheme will probably need to be a rather formal process too, with clear guidelines, a fixed timetable, the appraiser being firmly in control of the process and so on. It might be argued that in circumstances like these, the appraisal should be an important vehicle in organisational development, helping to change the organisation in the direction of greater flexibility. While this may, indeed, be the case, there is a danger that if it departs too rapidly and radically from the existing culture, it will be rejected. An example of how appraisal was designed and, over time, gradually modified to suit the culture is given in Box 5.2.

---

**Box 5.1: An example of consultation and participation in the design of a company appraisal scheme**

A motor manufacturer set up its own systems company, which decided to establish a new appraisal scheme to reflect its particular needs and circumstances. The principal consideration was to involve as many staff as possible in the design stage, not only to gain commitment but to draw upon their extensive experience of appraisal in the past.

A series of discussion groups, each consisting of 12 employees representing a cross-section of staff from differing divisions, organisational levels and occupational groups, was set up. Each group considered the need for an appraisal system and how present practices could be improved. Amongst the conclusions of these discusssions were:

- performance should be measured against agreed objectives
- elements of self-appraisal should be included
- the overall performance rating should be dropped
- the employee development element of the system should be kept separate from the appraisal of performance element.

The next stage was to draft an appraisal form and procedure that conformed to the groups' requirements. The personnel department, which had taken the lead in facilitating the consultation process, then presented the provisional scheme to senior management and staff unions as the basis for appraisal over a trial period. Despite some reservations, this was agreed. The four-month trial took place, and all appraised under the new system were asked for their views through questionnaires and interviews. The reactions were very favourable, though there were some suggestions for changes (in relation to details rather than the overall approach) that were incorporated in the final version of the scheme. This was accepted by senior management and staff unions and put into operation (Scott, 1983). It ran successfully for many years after that.

---

---

**Box 5.2: Evolving appraisal practices to match changes in the Civil Service culture**

When a comprehensive performance appraisal scheme was introduced for the first time into the UK Civil Service in the early 1970s (Anstey, Fletcher and Walker, 1976), the approach taken was carefully suited to the culture. It was a closed scheme, where the general standing of the appraisee as regards performance and potential could be discussed in the interview, but the actual ratings were not disclosed; in fact, none of the lengthy written report, apart from the agreed job description, was seen by the appraisee. The emphasis was on discussing performance in the light of detailed ratings of job-relevant qualities. The appraisee was invited to complete a preparation form before the appraisal interview, but this was not part of the record of the event.

Looking back now, this appears to be a rather formal and even paternalistic way of going about appraisal. However, in the context of the time and the stage of development of the organisation, it represented a significant move forward that did not shift too far away from the existing culture. It broke new ground by implementing a standard approach to appraisal, based on training the appraisers, that led to face-to-face job discussions between managers and subordinates. Given that no such discussions had taken place previously, it would have been asking too much too quickly for appraisers to be required to take on a more open form of appraisal, incorporating elements of self-appraisal and objective-setting.

Once started, however, the appraisal system – along with other changes – paved the way for a rather more contemporary style of management and a different approach to appraisal. Over the years, the Civil Service appraisal system has become a more open, participative and flexible one. Looking at it now, it would be difficult to see any traces of the original scheme. With the introduction of objective-setting and (more recently) PRP, it looks more like the kind of appraisal scheme found in many business organisations, and as such is perhaps an indicator of how the Civil Service culture itself has changed.

---

With the numerous changes and pressures of recent times, many organisations have shifted to a style and structure that a few years ago would only have been found in advanced technology and computing companies. The delayering process has removed several levels of management; greater autonomy and profit/loss accountability has been given to the individual operating units; the demand for speed in responding to market changes has increased (often necessitating changes in staffing and organisation, with more use of matrix management), and so on. Partly as a result of this, the power base of managers has changed and now often stems from their demonstrated expertise and competence as opposed to being legitimised simply by their rank in the hierarchy.

In circumstances such as these, a flexible and adaptable approach to appraisal is necessary, with a greater degree of local control over content and administration − much as was described in the context of performance management in the last chapter. This usually fits in well with appraisal that is primarily geared to motivation and development and has a high level of appraisee participation. But where assessment and comparison comes into the picture as the focus for appraisal, difficulties arise. The use of standard report formats and rating scales, completed at fixed times by the nominated appraising manager to facilitate cross-company comparison, does not sit comfortably within the framework of organisations geared to flexibility and quick reaction.

Even within a single organisation there can be marked variations in culture and attitude, however. An example of this will be found in quite a few local authorities, where the response of the social services department and of the highways department to what is ostensibly the same appraisal scheme frequently differ in ways that reflect aspects of the staff groups involved. The former has a strong social work ethos, with considerable emphasis on interpersonal issues, and so handling the appraisal interview process in an open but sensitive way becomes paramount. The latter department, whose staff are often professionally qualified engineers and the like, tend to have quite a different attitude. They are inclined to concentrate more on any quantitative elements in the scheme (which are usually to be found in the paperwork) and are usually stronger on directness than on subtlety in the communication process. Other departments that differ in terms of functions and staff make-up could just as easily exhibit these and other variations of response to appraisal. No doubt much the same is also true in some divisions of private sector organisations.

How can these cultural differences be allowed for when devising the appraisal scheme? Again, the use of a core appraisal scheme with additional elements added locally to meet specific needs and to increase its relevance is one option. Any good consultation process should bring to light what variations are needed. However, it is not always the case that the scheme itself has to be modified. In the example given above of the social work and highways departments, the problem is perhaps more one of orienting the training and presentation of the scheme to address the likely differences in attitudes, reactions and skills. There are, of course, other cultural variations of a rather different nature that are found within organisations. The ethnic and national mix of employees is becoming more heterogeneous, and the concept of managing diversity has growing significance for performance appraisal. Again, however, this subject relates at least as much to training as to design, and it will be discussed later in Chapter 6.

One of the effects of delayering has been to produce flatter management hierarchies. Some organisations have had this kind of structure for years anyway, and it does bring with it a problem for conventional appraisal systems. The norm has been for the individual's immediate boss to do the appraisal, with some input from the 'grandparent' – the boss two levels up. This becomes a less practicable arrangement when the structure of the management hierarchy means that each manager has many direct reports. The precise number that any one appraiser can manage is a favourite topic for taxing the minds of those trying to design and implement appraisal systems. There is of course no definitive answer to this question, and much depends on the timing – are all the appraisals to be done in a rather limited period, or can they be spread through the year? Assuming a restricted time limit and the requirement that the appraisals be done properly, a rough guide is one per week, with a maximum of, say, 12 in eight weeks. That said, though, the situation often found now means that working to those figures would leave a lot of appraisals not done.

The problem is further compounded in many instances by the geographical spread of the organisation. With fewer management levels, and greater internationalisation of businesses, the appraisee's immediate boss can increasingly be based in another part of the country, or in another country altogether. It thus becomes very difficult for a manager in this position to be in full command of the facts about his subordinates' performance and development needs. All this leads to the next crucial question to be considered in designing appraisal schemes – who is the appraiser?

## Who Should Appraise?

The rationale advanced for the traditional, one-up appraisal is that the immediate boss is in the best position to assess and guide subordinates, because of the amount of contact and greater experience. However, as we have seen, the contact argument does not always hold good. Moreover, the concerns about the appraisers' objectivity and fairness in assessment have made this model problematic. One of the ways in which appraisal has been modified over recent years is the introduction of people other than the immediate boss into the process. The various alternatives that have been tried are outlined below.

### Self-appraisal

Over the last quarter of a century, there has been a pervasive increase in the degree to which appraisal systems have been structured to allow and encourage participation by the appraisee. Initially, it was limited to giving the individual a form to assist in preparing for the appraisal, listing headings that formed an agenda for the appraisal interview and inviting the person to think about them beforehand. This moved on to including sections on the report form for the appraisee to add their own comments on the appraisal, and to register any disagreement if necessary. Eventually, some organisations adopted an appraisal process that involved both appraiser and appraisee completing nearly identical appraisal forms, discussing them in an interview, and filing a single agreed report on the basis of this.

There are numerous advantages to incorporating self-appraisal into the appraisal process. It is said to engender more commitment on the part of the person appraised, because of its participative nature. It reduces defensiveness by encouraging the appraisees to take the lead in reviewing their own performance, rather than having an assessment imposed on them. It encourages appraisees to think about their own performance and development needs in a focused way. And by giving the perspective of two people – the appraiser and the appraisee – it should lead to more objective assessment than if it rested on either one alone.

It is not surprising, then, that self-appraisal has become so popular. But there are some problems that inhibit its use. Possibly the greatest of these is the danger of inflated or excessively lenient self-assessments. This can certainly happen, sometimes through a fundamental lack of objectivity on the part of the appraisee, sometimes because the situation is not one that motivates the individual to be accurate, and sometimes because the nature of the exercise does not facilitate accurate self-assessment. Research (Shrauger and Osberg, 1981; Mabe and West, 1982) suggests that while there are individual differences in self-assessment objectivity, on average people have the capacity to be reasonably accurate in reporting on their own behaviour. Whether they will deploy that capacity is another matter, though. If the motivational context of the situation is such that immediate decisions on rewards depend on it, then it is likely to strain anyone's objectivity and honesty, and people will be more inclined to be lenient in their self-assessments. Finally, if the invitation to self-assess is not framed appropriately, then it can promote inaccuracy. The latter is likely to arise when people are asked to compare themselves with others, especially if the others concerned are not all that familiar to them. It is often the case that people simply don't have the information to gauge their effectiveness against that of colleagues and peers and asking someone to make this kind of comparison is giving them a task they are likely not to be able to do very well.

All this serves to suggest that self-appraisal will do best where:

- the immediate boss does not see enough of the appraisee to be left as the only source of the appraisal data
- there are no reward decisions based solely on the outcome of the appraisal process
- the nature of the self-assessment is such that appraisees compare themselves against their own individual standards, and not against other people's standards.

This last point needs some elucidation. One of the most effective ways of using self-appraisal is to ask the person appraised to assess their performance against what they see as their own 'norm'. Thus, they might be invited to say what they feel they have done best and least well over the last year, or — in a more specific form — which of various listed attributes or competencies they feel themselves to be strongest on and weakest on. For example, an individual may rate himself high on information collection and handling but low on delegating to subordinates, but the high rating does not imply that this person is better than average in the department, nor does the low rating imply being worse than average – they both reflect variations against that appraisee's notional individual standard. Used in this way, self-appraisal has been found to be more discriminating and less subject to halo effect than appraisal done by others (Williams, 1989). An example of a scheme incorporating a strong element of this approach to self-appraisal is given in Appendix A.

Self-appraisal probably has the greatest potential in an appraisal system geared primarily to motivation and development. None the less, it is likely to be important in any type of appraisal system, since the individual's self-assessment will be on the agenda implicitly, if not explicitly, and it is better that it is overtly brought into play in some fashion as part of the process. Self-appraisal, like most things, can probably be taken too far, though. There is no more value in basing appraisal exclusively on the appraisees' views than there is on the appraisers', so it is unlikely that schemes that seek to do this will be very effective. The author came across one such appraisal scheme in an airline company, and found that the output from the appraisal process appeared to be ignored in all personnel decision-making – a sure sign that it was not taken seriously.

## Peer appraisal

The involvement of peers in the appraisal process is not something that has, as yet, become popular. It has an appeal in academic and teaching institutions, where there is often a dislike of formal hierarchical management structures. In universities, it is commonly an important input to promotion decisions, external assessors being asked to comment on the candidates' work and its impact on the field. But as an element in the assessment of performance on a shorter time scale, it has seldom been employed.

In theory, it should have a lot to offer, as peers may be in a position to give a unique insight into an individual's team contribution – no small concern when there is pressure for people to achieve that might sometimes lead them to put their own concerns ahead of the team effort. In fact, peer rating in general is not all that accurate or unbiased, judging from the research evidence (Kane and Lawler, 1978). This does not mean that it cannot be developed and effective ways found of utilising it as part of the appraisal process. The biggest stumbling block is likely to be the administrative one — the time it takes to collect peer ratings would add substantially to the work load involved in appraisal. There is also the danger, mentioned by Williams (1989), that peer involvement in appraisal could cause friction and disrupt team harmony.

For the moment, then, peer appraisal is more theory than practice. It needs more research and development work. We will return to it later in the context of appraising professional groups (Chapter 9).

## Multi-level, multi-source appraisal

This consists of a combination of self, peer and manager appraisal. One of the few documented examples of such an approach is that adopted on an experimental basis by Gulf Oil some years ago (Stinson and Stokes, 1980). This was designed to be additional to the existing appraisal scheme, and was limited to 30 senior managers in a number of countries; as noted above, geographical spread makes it hard for any one appraiser to monitor subordinates' performance effectively. Each member of this group chose between five and eight appraisers at any level who they felt were in a position to make a valid assessment of their performance. The appraisers so chosen completed the appraisal forms anonymously, then sent them to the HR department. The latter drew up a summary for the individual concerned, who prepared a self-appraisal in light of it. The appraisee's boss was also given the summary to help in preparing for the appraisal, which then took place. In general, this multi-source appraisal was well-received by all concerned.

In theory, multiple levels and sources of appraisal data should lead to a more objective, well-rounded picture of the individual's contribution, strengths and development needs. It should consequently promote higher levels of trust in the fairness of the process. There are, however, two main problems that are probably responsible for there being such limited use of this method. The first is that it is time-consuming and administratively rather cumbersome to run for anything but a very limited number of appraisees; the Gulf Oil example gives some indication of this. The second is that allowing people to choose who makes an input to their appraisal can offer an opportunity for the more Machiavellian to bias the process by arranging a reciprocal process of back-slapping. Whether this actually happens, at least in any significant proportion of cases, is not known.

Despite these drawbacks, real or potential, there does seem to be more scope for the use of some element of multiple-source appraisal (indeed, it has now been introduced into teacher appraisal; see Chapter 9). The Gulf Oil idea of making it an additional input to the normal appraisal process, rather than resting everything on it, seems to be a good one. Perhaps one way round the additional burden the method imposes is to only add this element every other year or so, or for the first year or two after taking up a new position. And to avoid the possible biasing effect of appraisees choosing their own raters, the latter could be agreed by both the appraiser and the appraisee. Hopefully, more organisations might experiment with this approach in the future; it has considerable promise as a development process.

## Appraisal by superiors

This heading does not refer to the traditional one-up appraisal process, but to the situation where the individual, over the course of the appraisal period, has had several bosses all of whom may contribute to the appraisal. It is, like peer appraisal, multi-source but not multi-level, and it is becoming increasingly common. The reason for its growing popularity is that, with the changes in organisational structure mentioned earlier, matrix management has become more prevalent. Where an individual works on a series of different projects over a year, serially or simultaneously, each with different project leaders, it becomes very difficult to identify any one person who should be the appraiser. The two approaches that most often find favour here are either to have a series of separate, project-specific appraisals, or to have one appraisal at the end of the review period where all those who have managed the individual contribute. The former has some merit, but it does suffer from the lack of an overall view; it is quite likely that an individual will vary in performance (or, more accurately, be seen to) from one project to another, not least because of the different team make-up and the relationships that result. The alternative method has more to recommend it; a manager is nominated to collect the appraisal information from all the individual's team/project leaders through the year and to base the appraisal on that. If there are any reward implications, then again it is easier to deal with on an overview basis. There is, of course, nothing to prevent there being informal review sessions with individual managers at the end of each project as well.

## Upward appraisal

Finally, and on a rather different note, there is the issue of upward appraisal; not so much a question of who should appraise, as who should appraise whom. There is some scope for upward appraisal in the multi-level/source appraisal already discussed, though there it is slightly diluted by being just one of several sources of feedback. Also, in the example given, it was provided anonymously (though there does seem to be a high probability of being able to guess the source if the appraisee has been allowed to nominate the raters in the first place!). A rather more direct form of upward appraisal is where this takes place in the context of the subordinate's appraisal review. Many organisations have, for some years, included some very mild gestures in this direction in the form of headings on the appraisees' preparation form that invited them to identify things that 'management' could do to help them improve performance. Recently, some UK organisations have taken this further. One major oil company, for example, has included an item on the preparation form that asks the appraisee to identify occasions in the last year on which the appraiser could have provided them with more support. Putting an item of this kind on the appraisal agenda seems to be a reasonable and perhaps not-too-threatening a step in the right direction.

Amongst the UK organisations currently using upward appraisal to at least a limited extent are W H Smith, BP Exploration, American Express and Rank Xerox. Two of these schemes are described briefly in Box 5.3; as will be seen, they are really supplementary to the normal appraisal process. However, the practice is much more widespread in the USA. For an excellent and thorough review of the topic, see Redman and Snape (1992), who suggest that upward appraisal has the advantages of both facilitating the empowerment of employees and making appraisal decisions more defensible against legal challenge (because they are based on a wider assessment input).

---

**Box 5.3: Two examples of upward appraisal**

Quite a lot of media attention has been given to the upward appraisal of managers in W H Smith and in BP Exploration (Falconer, 1991; Gapper, 1991; Summers, 1991). In W H Smith, survey data showed that managers were viewed by staff as being better at decision-making than at motivating subordinates. In the light of this, the company asked staff to rate their managers on 32 attributes. These included such things as:

- Communicates relevant information to me
- Plans out work effectively
- Inspires me to do well
- Does not impose unrealistic objectives
- Is courteous.

The ratings were done on a questionnaire, which was then mailed back to a source independent from the company for data analysis. They compiled a report for each manager, based on all the responses received (individual respondents were not identified). About 300 senior managers, nominated by their own bosses, were covered by this process. Any who had been in the job for less than three months or who had less than three subordinates were excluded.

The results of this exercise revealed that managers were often weak on interpersonal skills. They scored higher on decision-making and discipline than on motivating, listening, and developing staff. The feedback from this upward appraisal was used to plan training and development programmes for the managers concerned. There are four important points to observe about the W H Smith scheme:

- they went to some trouble to pilot it first
- steps were taken to make it as non-threatening as possible (full briefings, encouraging managers to hand out the questionnaires to their staff themselves, etc.)
- the output from it was not linked to pay
- it was a separate exercise from the normal appraisal process.

The company intend to repeat the process, with some

modifications, in the future, and are under pressure from middle managers to include them. The general reaction and resulting behaviour change seem to have been very positive.

The approach taken in BP Exploration is rather similar. It involves staff completing a questionnaire listing 23 management practices, rating their bosses on each of them. They include such items as 'accurately representing the views, opinions and feelings of staff up the line' and 'willingness to share power in the interest of common goals'. As in the previous example, the questionnaires go to an outside consultancy who produce a report for each manager. The consultants then go through the findings with the individual concerned. Following this, action plans are agreed in collaboration with the person's staff and boss. Although there is no link with pay at present, it is possible that there will be in the future.

What are the issues in considering how to include an element of upward appraisal in an appraisal scheme? The main ones seem to be:

- Frequently voiced concerns are that either the managers being appraised will feel their position to be undermined and react badly, or that their subordinates will not be frank enough to make any meaningful comments, or both. The managers may fear that subordinates could use the opportunity to exercise grudges, while the subordinates may fear some retaliatory punitive action by the managers. If high levels of mutual trust exist, such problems may not arise, but it seems mutual trust is more the exception than the rule. Thus, most upward appraisal schemes involve anonymity for the subordinates, their observations being collected and represented in summary form by some other party, as in the examples presented in Box 5.3. That other party can be the appraised person's boss, an external consultant or the personnel department. The latter two have the virtue of maintaining a higher level of subordinate anonymity. The use of upward appraisal data should, of course, be included in the appraisers' training.
- Given that there may be a degree of suspicion about the content of upward appraisal, it has to be based on a large enough sample to ensure that it is valid and that the individual sources cannot

be identified. A minimum of four or five subordinates is usually suggested, but some companies have eight or more. The implications for the time and administrative effort involved are clear.

- It is very unlikely that subordinates can comment equally accurately and appropriately on all aspects of their managers' performance. The managers themselves will have views on what their subordinates can usefully appraise, and this has to be taken into account if they are to accept the feedback in a constructive manner. The most obvious areas for upward appraisal are those relating to the management of staff (delegation, giving feedback, communication skills, goal-setting, etc.). With these, it is arguable that subordinates are in at least as good a position as the managers' own bosses to make an assessment. It is essential, though, that the managers appraised do have a major say in what is appraised by subordinates.
- The form of the appraisal by subordinates is also important. It can be ratings, free-written comments, or questionnaires. The best results are likely, as in any kind of appraisal, where the instructions and the task are made as clear as possible. So, any ratings will benefit from being behaviourally based and defined.

There are some circumstances where upward appraisal will either definitely not work or is very unlikely to. Where there has been little or no history of appraisal of any kind, it will represent too radical a step; it needs to come as part of a logical process of evolution in appraisal, preceded by an element of self-appraisal. It will encounter much more resistance where pay or promotion decisions are directly affected by the appraisal. And it cannot be used very readily where the individual has only one or two subordinates. Where there are no subordinates, it cannot take place. This last point states the obvious, but it does serve to illustrate a potential inequity here – if upward appraisal is not feasible for some people, then it does mean that the basis of appraisal is going to differ between managers, with some having subordinate input and some not. This should not be much of a problem, if the upward appraisal is centred on aspects of performance that are specifically related to managing subordinates, as it will only occur for those that have them.

Upward appraisal has been quite well received by managers in the USA (McEvoy, 1988, 1990), although this does not auto-matically mean that it will be in the UK. The appraisal literature suggests that there is less directness in communicating evaluations in Britain than in the USA, where directness is more the accepted norm. None the less, upward appraisal looks like being one of the main developments in this field in the UK in the 1990s. Because it can be a considerable burden in resource terms, it may deter many organisations from using it as a constant element in the appraisal. Amongst the alternatives open to them are to use it as an occasional additional input (as suggested earlier in relation to multi-source appraisal), or to make it voluntary (the danger with the latter is that those most in need may be those least likely to volunteer). It would be unfortunate if its reliance on rating scales encouraged a swing back to a predominantly assessment-oriented approach to ap-praisal, as its main benefit would appear to be as a development tool.

For the moment, upward appraisal is more talked about than practised in the UK, and so there is little in the research literature to guide us as to its likely impact. In the less hierarchical, more flexibly structured and knowledge-based organisations of the future, upward appraisal may find more of a place; it may need to. If it is to involve the personnel department as the collecting point for the data, then to avoid appraisals going back to being cumbersome, centrally administered, bureaucratic procedures, upward appraisal might best be used as a development activity that runs alongside the normal appraisal process on an intermittent or *ad hoc* basis.

## In conclusion

Although the practice of having appraisals done by the employees' immediate boss is still the norm, it is not likely to remain so to the same extent. All the influences identified earlier dictate that appraisal will become a more diversified process, quite possibly with different appraiser arrangements for different people in the organisation, according to their circumstances. This in turn has implications for training in appraisal; the necessary skills may need to be spread more widely within an organisation, and conveyed earlier in an individual's career than they are now.

## Who Should be Appraised?

One of the trends of the 1980s was that the coverage, in terms of staff groups, of appraisal schemes grew at both ends of the scale (Long, 1986). More than half the organisations surveyed by the IPM included directors in their appraisal schemes, and clerical, secretarial, skilled and semi-skilled workers were increasingly being drawn into the appraisal arrangements. So the answer to the question of who should be appraised is, in the view of many organisations – everybody. Long (1986) suggests that there are numerous reasons for this, including the desire to promote flexible working practices and increasing consistency in the conditions of management and non-management staff. The advent of performance management has given this trend a further boost, and PRP policies have also been applied to wider bands of staff.

The extension of appraisal schemes to take in more categories and levels of employees does not imply that it is the same scheme for all. There is some virtue in uniformity, but not a lot. An example of how the desire for bureaucratic convenience and similarity of assessment can be taken to extremes is provided by an appraisal report form used in many government departments in the early 1970s. This form required all staff – from nuclear physicists to clerical officers, from first level supervisors to senior managers – to be rated on the same set of dimensions. The notion that the same attributes were relevant to such a wide range of jobs is quite ludicrous. The same *elements* of appraisal may be present in the appraisal scheme at different levels, in the sense that there may be some objective-setting and assessment of some job-related abilities, but the form and content of them should certainly vary to suit the circumstances. For instance, in jobs which allow for little personal discretion in determining work style and output, there may be limited scope for setting personal targets, in which case the results-oriented aspect of the appraisal would be diminished. For some unskilled and routine tasks, the purpose of the appraisal may be limited to simply acknowledging the part played by the individual and listening to any problems, views or ideas they want to raise. In the case of younger and more inexperienced staff, self-appraisal may be less helpful and appropriate as a method as they may have difficulty in judging their own performance at this stage.

So, performance appraisal has something to offer for all

categories and levels of staff, but it is not the same in every case. The implication is that the organisation needs not one, but two or three schemes that share some common thinking and components and which are tailored to the needs of the level or group concerned. It is important, though, to try to ensure that no staff group end up feeling that they are being treated as second-class citizens on the basis of different appraisal processes. A medium-sized county council found that when it had PRP for senior levels and not for the management grades immediately beneath, the latter felt that they were missing out in some way, and that they were earning their bosses' pay rises.

## The Administration of Appraisal

There are three main aspects to this that will be discussed here — frequency, documentation and timing. A fourth one, the monitoring and maintenance of appraisal schemes, will be looked at later in Chapter 7.

### Frequency

With the predominance of results-oriented appraisal, what was formerly the most usual practice of holding appraisals annually makes less sense. The problem is that objectives are so susceptible to changing circumstances, and progress against them needs to be reviewed more frequently than just once a year. Consequently, many organisations have a formal review and objective-setting session annually, but encourage the appraisers to hold interim reviews either quarterly or half-yearly. Apart from checking that objectives are still relevant, these also provide the opportunity to take remedial action if the appraisee is having difficulties. No additional paperwork need be involved in interim reviews, though any changes may have to be added to the original statement of agreed objectives.

The periodicity of appraisals may vary for other reasons, too. For *some* older staff nearing retirement, it may be that appraisals — or some elements of them — are less meaningful. They might be given the choice of opting out for a year, though not more than that. On the other hand, with younger staff who are new to the job or to the organisation, there is arguably a need for an appraisal session within the first six months and two in the first year.

## Documentation

The one golden rule is to keep it to a minimum. The success of appraisal lies not in the paperwork but in the aims and attitudes of the participants. Like most things, this can be taken too far. There is a need for adequate background documentation to explain the scheme when it is launched, and for a sufficient formal record of the appraisal discussion and outcomes. The former will be dealt with when appraisal training is covered in Chapter 6. As far as the rest is concerned, the nature of the forms obviously depends on the scheme itself, but having something for the appraisee to work from, an agenda at very least (if no other self-appraisal is involved), is usually found to be necessary for a constructive session (Fletcher and Williams in IPM, 1992). The record of the appraisal has to be enough to give a clear picture of the main objectives and action points agreed when it is looked at in a year's time. What it does not have to do is to try to give a blow-by-blow account of the discussion, or to go into much detail. This kind of appraisal record usually generates more trouble than it is worth, and often reduces the appraisal to a kind of tortuous drafting session, with more emphasis on the formal record than on the substance of the discussion.

Who should actually hold copies of the appraisal forms also depends on the nature of the scheme. If the appraisal data is to be part of the process of determining pay and promotion, then usually it has to be made available to the personnel department. For appraisal where the focus is more on objective-setting and review, there may only be a need for the appraiser and appraisee to keep copies, though it is useful for there to be some notification to personnel that the event has taken place. Also, the manager two levels up should perhaps have a sight of the appraisal report to keep in touch with what is going on – though sometimes the sheer volume of appraisees militates against this. In general, the principle of restricting access to appraisal data to those who have an immediate need to see it is the one usually followed.

Turning to a very different aspect of the paperwork, there is no law that states that appraisal forms must be designed to look about as visually appealing as an income tax return. Given the need for brevity — nobody wants to see six-page blockbusters landing on the desk waiting to be completed on each appraisee — it is probably worth getting some professional help in the actual lay-out and presentation of the form. The appraisal paperwork should be professional in appearance (i.e. visually pleasing without being distracting), economical in its use of space, and effective in generating the information required. To leave nothing to chance, though, it is important to pilot all the appraisal paperwork on some appraisers and appraisees. The aim is not to check whether the system will work — piloting the system as a whole is a nice idea, but is seldom viewed as feasible — but just to ensure that what is said is understandable by the participants and can be used as is intended by them.

## Timing

When appraisals should take place is not always easy to decide. The preferred pattern has been for them all to be done within a limited period, partly for administrative reasons; all the forms can be sent out together, all the information sought by personnel can be collected at once. The disadvantage of this is that the load on appraisers is concentrated over just a few weeks, leaving them little time for anything else and probably feeling a bit jaded by the end of the process, too. It also does not necessarily match well with varying individual circumstances; an appraisee may have started the job only a few weeks before, or it may be that the appraiser is new to the position. For these reasons, some organisations have chosen to ask for appraisals to be done on the anniversary of the appointment to the current post, or have staggered them through the year on some other basis.

The balance, however, has swung towards the set-period approach. The reason for this is the tying-in of appraisal with other aspects of performance management. If the objectives set in appraisal are to link with the wider team and organisational objectives, if they are to relate to the business plan as a whole, then inevitably the appraisal process has to occur at a time that coordinates with these. The implication is that objective-setting will take place fairly soon after the business plan for the year has been laid down, and — where PRP is a feature of the situation — that the review of people's progress against objectives and the reward decisions arising out of it are made at a point when the results for the previous year are known (because the reward decisions generally rest on the amount of funds available for distribution in this form). If the organisation holds a separate appraisal session to focus on development needs, this can be timed with rather more flexibility.

## Chapter 6

# Training and the implementation of appraisal

The role of training in determining the success of an appraisal scheme cannot be over-estimated. Fletcher and Williams (1992) have shown how the effectiveness of performance appraisal is related to the training effort put into it by the organisations concerned. One of the most positive indicators of companies' attitudes to appraisal is that by the mid-1980s a far greater proportion of them (the majority, in fact) offered training in appraisal to their staff than had previously been the case (Long, 1986). Unfortunately, this does not mean that the training was taken up by all appraisers, nor does it say anything about the quality of the training. On both these criteria, there is great room for improvement. One of the main failings of appraisal training in the past has been the emphasis on the procedure and paperwork rather than on the process and the skills needed to carry out appraisal in a sensitive and constructive manner. It is, of course, important that everyone knows what the scheme consists of and how it is to be operated, but this is really the easy part. Because it has a high 'comfort factor', there is a tendency to focus on the report forms etc. as if they were the main purpose of the exercise, which they are not.

Most of this chapter will concentrate on how the behavioural skills needed in appraisal can be imparted. We will also consider the training needs of the appraisees. Before that, however, it is worth addressing the issue of where to start the ball rolling. The conventional wisdom seems to be right – to introduce appraisal at the top and to work down, on the basis that (a) top management have to be seen to be taking it seriously, and (b) it is a salutary experience for someone to have been appraised before they themselves appraise anyone else. There is some evidence to support the first contention. A recent review study by Rodgers and Hunter (1991) has demonstrated the importance of senior management involvement, though in the context of MBO schemes rather than appraisal as such. It found that organisations introducing MBO with a high level of senior management commitment achieved average productivity gains of over 56 per cent, compared to average gains of just over 6 per cent in the case of organisations where such commitment was lacking. By analogy, since more appraisal schemes now take in director-level staff, there is reason to hope that the commitment will be present.

## Background Briefing and Documentation

This element of appraisal training can be run as part of the appraisers' skills course or as a separate, preliminary session (the advantage of the latter is that it allows for larger groups to be dealt with at any one session than would be possible on a skills course). Its purpose is to tell all the appraisers what the thinking behind the appraisal scheme is, what it is trying to achieve, how it is structured and implemented, and to introduce and explain the forms and paperwork. If there has been a good consultation process in developing the scheme, then all this will be that much easier to put across. Without it, the sessions will probably take longer to run as there will need to be more time allowed to raise questions, allay anxieties and debate issues. In these cases, the briefing session is actually doubling as a commitment-gaining exercise. The aim is not just to inform but to sell the scheme to the appraisers.

The briefing sessions should normally be held fairly shortly before the appraisal training courses (if these are separate) and the first round of appraisals. It is often helpful to start by giving a short description of the recent history of appraisal in the organisation, and why there has been a need to change and/or to develop the new scheme. The aims of the new scheme and how it is to be operated can then be outlined. Either at the start of the session, or at this point, many organisations ask a member of top management to speak briefly in support of the appraisal scheme, to indicate high-level commitment to it and to emphasise that it is a worthwhile activity. It is not uncommon to find organisations inviting some external speaker — often a consultant or a prominent academic in the field — to make an input here as well. Their role is again to reassure the participants that the scheme is a good one and to draw some lessons from elsewhere (such as prestige, high-performing organisations) as to the value of effective performance appraisal. It is worth reiterating that if a genuine consultation process has allowed appraisers and appraisees to have a say in the design of the appraisal system, much of this selling effort will be unnecessary.

Something that can make life more or less difficult here is the way the briefing groups are made up. If any control can be exercised over this, it is probably best if any appraisers who are known to have particularly negative attitudes to appraisal and who can be very defensive about it – sometimes dubbed the 'awkward squad' – are spread round the groups. This way, their influence can be diluted and they may even be swayed to a more positive approach by their peers. If they are allowed to collect in one group, however, they usually just reinforce each other's prejudices and fears. The other question about group composition is whether it is better to make it representative of the organisation as a whole, by getting a cross-section of appraisers from different departments to each session, or to run separate sessions for each department or division. Each has its pros and cons, but if there is to be any kind of flexibility in the way the scheme operates to meet local needs, then the latter approach is clearly better.

The content of the briefing sessions varies according to how far they are intended to serve as part of the training proper. If they do have a function beyond informing and gaining commitment, then it usually involves taking the participants through any guidance notes that are issued and maybe giving some instruction on rating and report form completion. These topics will be dealt with below when the training itself is considered. Also, the question of briefing appraise*ees* will be covered later in the broader context of what training might be given to them.

## Training the Appraisers

It is not just the 'awkward squad' who are apprehensive about appraisal. Many managers do not have a great deal of confidence in their ability to handle appraisal interviews effectively, and so tend to cling to the paperwork. Some have an exaggerated idea of what appraisal involves and what it demands of them (this is especially true if they have little or no experience of it). They see the appraisal as being akin to professional counselling, and feel ill-equipped to take it on. Others try to reduce their anxieties by minimising the importance of appraisal, seeking to make it sound trivial or unnecessary. This usually gives rise to the kinds of comment every trainer who has run an appraisal course has heard umpteen times – 'This is only what I do on a day-to-day basis anyway', 'Good managers (i.e. me) don't need appraisal', etc. The implication is that appraisal is a superfluous and redundant addition to the dialogue that is already taking place. However, both research (Fletcher, 1978; Nathan, Mohrman and Milliman, 1991) and experience suggest very strongly that this is not true. It is precisely those managers who have frequent communications with their staff who have the most productive appraisals.

The extent of the appraisers' concerns about their ability to conduct the appraisal will depend on its content and aims, and how much say they have had in them. But even where they have participated fully in the design stage, there will still be a fair number who need to have their confidence built up through the training process. Training here is as much about giving that confidence as it is about teaching specific skills. For this reason, it is vital that:

- The training is organised so as to ensure that there is enough time for participants to see that they are capable of doing a good job. If there is time for just one practice session, the appraiser often does not handle it well and then has no opportunity to learn from the feedback and improve both performance and confidence.
- The training is delivered as close as possible to the time of the first appraisals.

Neither of these is very easy to arrange. The ratio of participants to trainers on any one course should not really rise above 4:1 if there is to be a supervised practical element and effective feedback. Unless the organisation has a lot of trainers, this means that it will take some while to train everyone. So those going through on the first courses might have some time to wait before conducting their appraisals, if the organisation is working on a common starting date and the principle that no-one will appraise unless trained to do so. In addition, the time commitment needed for good skills training makes it rather costly.

The time problem is particularly acute for senior managers, as it is difficult, if not impossible, to get them away from their desks for two days. There are two main options open to cope with this. First, the line of least resistance: run shorter courses for more senior and (in theory) more experienced people. The problem here is that they give the lead, and if they do not demonstrate their belief in the importance of the scheme, the message will get through to those below them. Also, being more senior and more experienced does not mean being more competent in handling appraisal. As has been observed on many occasions, 20 years' experience can often be one year's experience repeated 20 times. The better second option, if at all possible, is to try to break up the training for senior managers so that they can attend on a couple of separate sessions. There is another difficulty in delivering training to the most senior levels, though. Top managers are not noted for their willingness to expose any of their real or imagined failings in front of peers. As a result, skills training conducted by in-house trainers is often politically unacceptable at these higher levels. The only way round this is to either abandon the skills element altogether or, preferably, to find suitable externally-run, open courses pitched at senior management level.

## Assessment skills

Where the orientation of the appraisal scheme has a strong assessment component, this will need to be reflected in the training by:

- describing the dimensions on which the appraisees are to be assessed
- providing some exercises to help course participants to correctly identify the behaviours relevant to each dimension, and to assess them appropriately
- outlining some of the main rating/assessment errors.

The first of these seems straightforward enough, but is worth spending time on. How the dimensions were arrived at, and precisely what they mean, needs to be gone into fairly thoroughly. The less the detail given on the appraisal form, the greater the time needed to discuss the behaviours the dimensions are dealing with. Without this, the appraisers will work to different interpretations of the dimensions and the scale points on them. With BARS or similarly based assessment devices, there is much less danger of this.

Course participants usually find exercises in using the assessment dimensions extremely helpful. One type of exercise is to give them a pen picture of an individual and to ask them to complete the assessment ratings on the basis of this. The ratings are subsequently discussed with the trainers and other course members. Alternatively, they can be given a written list of behavioural observations and asked to decide which assessment dimension each one relates to. If the observations are quite detailed, they can be allocated a rating on the dimension as well. A step up from this is to present the course members with videos showing work episodes that illustrate the behaviours underlying the appraisal dimensions, then have them do the assessments on what they have seen. One advantage of this approach is that it can also be done on a distance learning basis; appraisers do not have to attend the course (or that element of it) at all.

The purpose of exercises of this kind is not only to ensure that appraisers gain a common understanding of what is being assessed and the standards involved, but that they also learn about some of the problems and pitfalls of assessment. At some point in the training process, they need to be made aware of the biases and distortions that can creep in. This can be put over in written form, and reinforced through the examples that arise — fortuitously or by design — in the course of doing the practical exercises. Some of the most frequent assessment errors and their sources are described in Box 6.1 below (another, prejudice and discrimination, will be discussed later). One final point about providing this kind of assessment training: experience suggests that it pays dividends even outside the immediate context of the appraisal, helping managers develop assessment skills they can use in a range of situations.

**Box 6.1: Sources of bias and error in assessment**

- *Halo effect.* This is the tendency to allow one or two favourable attributes of an individual to colour one's judgment of all their other attributes. The result is to produce an overall, rather un-discriminating positive assessment – a 'halo'. The opposite phenomenon is sometimes called the 'horns effect'; this is where some unfavourable attribute of the person appraised leads to a generally negative impression being formed. This kind or error is one of the most commonly encountered, in selection interviews as well as in appraisal.

- *Attributional error.* Before this is described, try a little exercise for yourself. Think of an incident recently where you did not perform as well as you would have hoped; why did this happen, how would you explain it? When you have mulled that over, move on to another incident, this time one where one of your subordinates (or, if you do not have any, a peer) did not perform as well as you hoped – again, why did this happen, how would you explain it? No cheating now; do not read on until you have analysed the two incidents!

  Have you displayed 'fundamental attributional error' (to give it its full name)? This refers to a pervasive tendency we all have to take much more account of the situational circumstances in explaining our own behaviour – especially when we have been less than successful – than we do in explaining other people's behaviour. When it comes to understanding why others have acted the way they did, we are much more likely to make dispositional attributions. In other words, we see other people's actions as being caused by their personality and abilities and we play down the importance of the situation, the context of the behaviour. The implications of this for appraisal are clear: the danger is that the appraiser will be too ready to see a lack of goal achievement as being due to the appraisee's deficiencies and will not make enough allowances for other factors (of which the appraiser may well be one).

- *Biased sampling.* There are two main forms of this. First, the tendency to base the appraisal on the last month or two of the period under review, because that is what dominates in the memory. Things that happened earlier, in what is the greater part of the appraisal period, are forgotten. The second form, which sometimes occurs in combination with the first, is to recall only the times when things have gone wrong, when the appraisee has not performed well. The extent to which this happens is demonstrated by the large number of people in organisations who work on the philosophy of 'no news is good news'.

- *Faulty implicit personality theory.* Most people, without being conscious of it, have some ideas about personality and how it is structured; they have an implicit personality theory that guides them, and which may not always be built on sound foundations. You can see this in how untrained assessors rate candidates in group exercises: the candidates who talk most easily are often judged as being the highest on emotional stability. Actually, there is no good reason for assuming that an articulate person is also a stable one, but although faulty, it is a common inference about personality. Another frequent error is to assume that an assertive individual is also more organised and more intellectually able than someone who is not. These kinds of ideas about personality traits and the relationship between them can be a source of distortion in the way appraisers assess their staff.
- *'Similar to me' effect.* This is very common in interviews and can affect appraisals, too. It is where a similarity in attitudes, preferences or background between the appraiser and appraisee influences the former to be positive in response to the latter, even to the extent of being unduly favourable in assessing performance. It is a kind of 'halo' effect, and one based on a very human tendency; similarity attracts – we are inclined to like people we see as being similar to ourselves.

## Appraisal interview training

The training given to cover the conduct of the interview itself needs to deal with a variety of skills required in:

- obtaining information
- giving feedback
- problem-solving
- motivating
- counselling.

For a full discussion of these skills, the reader is referred to Randell (1980) and Walker (1989). The focus here is chiefly on the kind of training that is necessary to impart process skills relevant to appraisal.

Many courses include a video or training film, either produced in-house or obtained from external sources, to illustrate teaching points. Some of these are very useful, not least in promoting discussion amongst the course members. However, they do need to be professionally made and presented to be really effective – amateurish efforts simply give the more sceptical amongst the audience further ammunition to ridicule the appraisal scheme. There is little doubt, though, that appraisal interview training can only really be tackled effectively through practical exercises where the participants get feedback on their performance from trainers and fellow course members. One of the most commonly used techniques is the role play interview. Typically, this involves one course member appraising another on the basis of a written brief that describes the situation and their different perspectives. An alternative is to ask the individual playing the role of the appraisee to base it on a real problem case known to them. However, this kind of exercise exacerbates the inevitable artificiality of the training situation, and allows the favourite escape clause of 'Well, of course, I would not have handled it that way in real life'.

A much better approach, and one that generates a higher level of realism and course member involvement, is to get the participants to perform a task that they are then appraised on by their fellow course members. There are a number of ways of doing this. They may work on a group project – often akin to an assessment centre group decision-making task – then appraise one another on their individual contribution and performance. Or, depending on the numbers involved and the time available, they may all be given a turn at leading the rest of their syndicate in a task (building structures from Lego bricks, etc.) and then be appraised on that. A third variation is to get one course member to give a short presentation on a topic, have a second one appraise them on that, the third participant appraises the second on the handling of the appraisal, and so on. There are as many permutations on the exercise theme as the trainers' imagination permits.

The point about exercises of this kind is that, whilst they only allow the appraisal of performance in one isolated event, they do offer an opportunity to practice appraisal skills on genuine behavioural examples. The course members are ego-involved to the extent that they find it a demanding task, with the minimum of artificiality. True, the nature of the task that they are appraised on is not specifically and directly job-relevant, but this is not a disadvantage – a task that is very complex or involved in the work of the organisation runs the risk of focusing too much attention on content and detracting from the real point of the exercise, which is about process.

The usual format in running such exercises is for the syndicate tutor to ask the appraiser and then the appraisee for their feelings and observations on how the practice interview was conducted, followed by feedback from the tutor and the other syndicate members. The latter may have been given some kind of checklist to guide their observations (see Appendix B for an example) and the tutor may divide the monitoring and feedback between them so that they individually concentrate on different aspects of the way the appraiser handled the session. Whichever way this is done, however, it provides another valuable opportunity to practice much the same feedback skills as are needed in an appraisal situation. This needs to be pointed out before the practice interviews commence, and some guidance given to course members on how to go about giving feedback to one another. Box 6.2 presents some general guidance on giving feedback in this context (and, indeed, on conducting an appraisal interview itself). More detailed guidance on feedback skills can be found in Egan (1990) and Slivinski and Bourgeois (1977). The value of having a course which permits each participant the chance of doing at least two practice interviews is that they have a chance to learn from the first and to improve their skill and confidence in the second.

---

**Box 6.2: Some general points on giving feedback**

The purpose of feedback is to help the person to whom it is directed. To this end, it should be given in such a way that the person (a) understands it, (b) accepts it, and (c) can do something about it. How can this be achieved? There are some general rules to follow that can help here:

- Be tentative – seldom are things so clear-cut that observations take on the mantle of indisputable fact, to be conveyed as such.
- Be concrete – discuss specific behaviours and examples to illustrate and support the points being made.

- Be respectful – try to communicate acceptance and understanding of the individual; you are talking about their performance of a task, not discussing their personality and values.
- Identify both the positive and the negative aspects of performance – resist the temptation to harp on the deficiencies alone.
- Be constructive – offer suggestions as to how the situation might have been tackled differently.
- Do not try to make too many critical points – apart from the danger of generating defensive reactions, people can only take in and deal with just so much at one time.
- Concentrate your observations on the aspects of performance that the individual can do something about – there is little sense in focusing on deficiencies that will be impossible for the person to remedy.
- Make sure your value judgments are identified as such, and not presented as facts.

Exercises of the kind described give the opportunity for practising skills in collecting information. The appraiser should be asking the right kind of questions to find out why the appraisee approached the task in the way they did, and so on. Skills can also be practised in giving feedback and, to an extent, in counselling on how to improve. The exercises may be a vehicle for demonstrating skill in problem-solving, though this will not necessarily be the case unless some deliberate effort has been made to build this in from the inception. Perhaps the one area in which they do not give adequate opportunity to develop skills is that of motivation. This is such a neglected topic in appraisal training that a separate section is devoted to it later in this chapter.

The practical component of an appraisal course needs to be supported with some written notes for guidance to reinforce the message conveyed in the training. These can be taken away and referred to by the appraisers to refresh their memories before they do their appraisals. An example of the kind of thing that might be given is presented in Appendix A. Apart from going over the basic points again, guidance notes can deal with issues that there may not be time for on the training course; for example, how to deal with special problem cases. There is an understandable desire amongst some attending appraisal courses to be told how to deal with every conceivable reaction and problem. Clearly, it is not possible to provide answers to this; the aim of the training is usually to impart generic skills and techniques that can be adapted and applied to a range of situations and needs. Course exercises normally focus on examples of typical appraisal content and interaction, since this is what most appraisers have to deal with most of the time. But there are extreme cases that occasionally arise — appraisees becoming overly emotional, or aggressive, or seeking to be manipulative, for example. The appraisers' concerns about these make them loom larger in their minds than the probability or frequency of them happening actually warrants. But they cannot be ignored. Even if they are the exception rather than the rule, when they *do* occur, they can cause the appraiser a disproportionate amount of trouble. If the time available for practical exercises is too limited to deal with them, then the alternatives are (a) to include some written advice on the handling of problem cases, (b) to provide advice through a video presentation — which can also be done on a take-away basis, and (c) provide a 'helpline' that appraisers can ring to seek advice, usually from the HR department.

One last point on the training of appraisers: it is valuable if they can be offered the opportunity to attend some kind of follow-up session run by training and/or personnel department staff. This might be in the nature of an 'appraisal clinic', where they bring back for discussion specific problems or issues that they have encountered in carrying out their interviews. It could also take the form of a review group made up of the original course membership convened at the end of the appraisal cycle where (for an hour or so) they can raise any particular difficulties and seek advice. Both of these serve a further purpose in acting as monitoring devices for the appraisal scheme as a whole.

## Training Appraisees

The notion of training appraisees is a relatively new one, and it is still far from commonplace. But it is a logical consequence of introducing elements of self-appraisal. If the appraisees are to have a significant input into the appraisal process, then they should be given some help in making it effective. It is also something that might be expected if the appraisees have been included in a consultation exercise about the nature of appraisal in the first place. Of course, many appraisers are, in their turn, appraised by their own bosses. For them, the appraiser training will probably fulfil most of the needs from the appraisee perspective, though a short session specifically focusing on this could be included in the appraisal interview course. It is no bad thing to give appraisers an opportunity to put themselves on the other side of the desk and see how things look from there.

Frequently, appraisee courses are simply briefing sessions, with no real practical component. They sometimes take place within the broader context of induction courses, and in contrast with appraiser courses, there is seldom any pressure to attend. One county council I spoke to had found that the take-up rate of places on appraisee courses was so low that they eventually withdrew them. This is rather disappointing and fairly unusual, perhaps caused by a lack of understanding of what was on offer. The content of appraisee training to some extent mirrors that of the appraisers. It can include the following:

- *Background briefing*. At very least, they need to know what the aims of the scheme are and how it is to run.
- *How to prepare*. This may be simply providing an agenda, or giving a preparation form, or it may include how to complete a self-appraisal form that is an integral part of the process.
- *Guidance on objectives*. This should encourage the appraisee to think in advance about what these might be for the year ahead, and give some training on how objectives should be framed.
- *Discussion of self-assessment*. This should look at the strengths and weaknesses of self-assessment, and review its place in appraisal.
- *Combating anxiety*. Interviews of all sorts create a degree of apprehension, and some cognitive-behavioural techniques (imaging, relaxation, etc.) for reducing anxiety can be taught where needed.
- *Assertiveness training*. Some basic guidance can be given to help appraisees put their own point of view across to a superior without being unduly emotional or defensive.
- *How to respond to criticism*. One of the concerns uppermost in appraisees' minds is the prospect of criticism and how they will

react − talking through the issues here can help them respond more constructively and confidently if and when it happens.

- *How to get action.* The appraisees can be encouraged to take the initiative in following up action recommendations to ensure that they are implemented.

Many of these can be presented in the form of discussion topics, though there is plenty of scope of practical exercises if desired. Training appraisees is something that can add a significant impetus to the effective running of an appraisal scheme, in that if they are empowered to drive it from their side, the appraisers will find it hard to do anything but respond with their best efforts.

## Other Issues in Appraisal Training

### Appraising diversity

Where appraisees and appraisers are from different cultural or ethnic groups, there can be the potential for misunderstanding and poor communication. A business services organisation I did some research on had found evidence of this and were trying to make sure that their new appraisal documentation was framed in language that was understandable to all. Piloting it with representatives of all the groups involved helps here. This is an issue that is worth sensitising appraisers to in training if they are likely to appraise staff of very diverse cultural backgrounds (or, indeed, educational levels). There are different styles of interpersonal communication and self-presentation that have been found to characterise different cultures. Hofstede (1980), for example, studied differences within IBM across over 40 countries and identified many variations, centring around such things as:

- the extent to which power was centralised or dispersed, with its implications for how authority is perceived and accepted
- the degree to which deviance from norms and values would be tolerated (e.g. less in Greece than in Sweden)
- the balance between individualism and collectivism (Australia being high on the former and Pakistan high on the latter).

These and other factors have an impact on individual behaviour. Individuals from, say, a Chinese background may not feel it appropriate to assert their views with superiors, as this is regarded as impolite within their culture. Appraisers dealing with culturally diverse groups – which now applies to many managers, not just those in international businesses – should have some part of their training focused on likely culturally based differences and the need to adapt appraisal style accordingly. For instance, it is possible that it will take considerably more effort to encourage self-appraisal and two-way communication with some groups, and the appraiser should be prepared for this. The training of appraisees is also important here. Many of the elements of appraisee courses listed earlier can be given special emphasis where the cultural mix indicates that it is likely to be needed.

Another aspect of having a diverse workforce is that it can produce the bias and prejudice that gives rise to unfair discrimination, on the grounds of race or sex. Whilst there is a need to monitor the output of appraisal schemes for this, there is also a need to tackle it from the other end, the input. Bias does not always show itself in the form of ratings or of the assessment of target achievement (if the latter is as objective as it is supposed to be, then there is hopefully less opportunity for this to happen). It can be more subtle than that, but just as damaging. Going back to the concept of attributional error, Garland and Price (1977) found that successful performance in female managers was attributed by prejudiced male managers to either luck or to the task being an easy one, whereas unprejudiced managers put it down to high ability and hard work. Similar distortions in the explanation of good or poor performance can arise where the appraisees are members of ethnic minorities and the appraisers are racially prejudiced.

This kind of bias can be illustrated in various ways. One approach is through assessment exercises – for example, appraisers can be given written descriptions of individuals and their performance and asked to react to them in some way (e.g. by rating the people described or explaining their likely motives for behaving the way they did). Half the appraisers can be given the description containing a female principal character and the other half given the same one but with a male character. Comparing the ratings and accounts of the two groups – without identifying individuals – often brings out into the open the kinds of stereotypes and assumptions that are part and parcel of bias. Needless to say, though, this requires especially sensitive handling on the part of the trainers. A less demanding strategy is to bring to appraisers' attention the findings of studies such as that carried out by the Tavistock Institute (HMSO, 1978) which found that non-white workers got more low performance ratings and fewer high performance ratings than their white counterparts, without being any more likely to have remedial training needs indicated on the appraisal forms.

Finally, one other mistake that male appraisers in particular need to be alerted to was identified by HR staff in a large local authority. This was a tendency to equate working late in the office with quality of work and commitment, which was then reflected in PRP recommendations. The most frequent losers from this were women who, having worked the full day, then went home to their families.

## Training to motivate

Many, perhaps most, appraisal schemes pay at least lip service to the aim of motivating those appraised. For some of them, it is one of their main purposes. Yet if you look at the content of appraisal training courses, you seldom find any mention of the word motivation. There seems to be an assumption that simply doing the appraisal is enough to motivate the appraisee, and if that is not the case, then it is down to the performance-related pay to do the job. What does motivate people at work, and how can this knowledge be built into appraisal courses?

There is no one, universally accepted theory of motivation that explains the differences between people in the effort and commitment they put into their work (for a good general introduction to this field, the reader is referred to Robertson, Smith and Cooper, 1992). The two main theories that have found favour and a fair amount of empirical support are Goal-Setting Theory and Expectancy Theory. The former deals mainly, as the name implies, with the motivating qualities of goal-setting and how to maximise them. The evidence – reviewed by Locke and others (1981) and Latham and Lee (1986) – shows over and over again how goal-setting is effective in raising performance levels. Few findings in occupational psychology are more reliable than this one – more than 90 per cent of all studies on goal-setting show positive effects. To elaborate a little further, this research shows that:

- More difficult and more clearly quantifiable goals encourage achievement to a greater extent than do easier and vaguer goals. Exhortations of the 'do your best' variety are of no value.
- For performance improvement to take place, there has to be adequate feedback on goal achievement – but feedback alone, without there being goals set (as one finds in many appraisal systems) does not lead to improvement.
- Commitment to the goals is necessary for the goals to affect performance, and that commitment is affected both by the expectations of success in achieving the goals, and by the value placed on that success.

The last of these points brings forward the other best-supported theory of work motivation, namely Expectancy Theory (Vroom, 1964; Locke and Henne, 1986). This stresses the need for individuals to be able to see a clear and positive relationship between the amount of effort they put in, the performance improvement it brings about, and the way that improvement leads to valued outcomes. Only if all these conditions are met is the individual likely to be fully motivated. Whilst appraisers cannot being about all of these conditions, they can play an important role in influencing them.

These two theories do not explain all work motivation, but together they offer a sound basis for moving forward. Any appraisal system that is intended to motivate would benefit from exposing appraisers to these concepts as part of the training, and inviting them to explore the implications for the appraisal scheme and what they as appraisers can do at the practical level to make the appraisal a motivating experience. This is where another ingredient needs to be added – consideration of individual differences. Following the broad principles of goal-setting and expectancy theories will be a good guide, but there is still the need to understand the make-up of the individual appraisee. When discussing the place of appraisal within a performance management framework (pages 42–43), it was noted that people vary greatly in what motivates them, and that different things were important to the same person at differing career stages. The appraiser needs to be aware of this, and to know what, in expectancy theory terms, are the outcomes the individual values. If the organisation runs an appraisal scheme that allows managers some latitude in dispensing rewards — and the emphasis here is at least as much on the non-financial variety as the financial — and the manager knows the appraisees well enough, then the appraisal process can be successful in motivating performance improvement. Appraisal training, then, can facilitate this by directing course members' attention to the nature of individual differences in this respect. Brain-storming some ideas about what rewards appraisees *and* the appraisers themselves value can be a useful course exercise that provides a basis for more creative thinking about appraisal as a motivational tool.

One last point here: most of what has been said about motivation in this section hinges on providing the impetus for improved performance through appraisal. Whilst it is important to include this as part of appraisal training, it also has to be emphasised in training that this alone is not enough. Motivating subordinates to improve is one thing, but without the empowerment and development to allow them to, not a lot will be achieved.

## Who does the training?

This used to be a fairly straightforward matter, and probably remains so for many organisations where appraisal falls directly into the lap of the personnel and training departments. Things are less simple, though, where appraisal is part of a performance management system and is owned by line management. If the latter have had some part — possibly a major one — in designing it, then they may also have some role in the training. The problem is that they may not be very good at training! Rather than abdicate this role to the line, the best solution may be for the HR department to work in collaboration with line representatives to tailor and deliver the training required by local circumstances. This can be through jointly designed and presented courses, or through a system of cascaded training, where HR staff train a cadre of line managers (self-nominated and/or nominated by local management) to go out and train their colleagues, providing them with the necessary back-up materials (OHP transparencies, handouts, and so forth). This group of managers can then adapt the basic package to the way appraisal operates in their own divisions. One of the advantages of this approach, reported by organisations that use it, is that these line managers — if they are well-chosen — have a high level of credibility with their colleagues, and are the most effective representatives for the appraisal scheme. The initial training provided for them by HR has to be of the highest standard, though; they have to go away convinced of the value of what they are doing if they are to gain the commitment of their colleagues.

On a rather different theme is the relative virtue of in-house versus bought-in training. At very senior levels, for reasons given earlier, it is often necessary to go outside the organisation to arrange suitable courses. For the rest, much depends on the training resources available. If there is no expertise in-house, then getting external help is the only option. This does not necessarily mean buying places on courses; it can be much better to hire a consultant to work with the organisation and run courses specifically for it. In fact, buying places on externally run public courses is probably the least attractive and least effective form of training. Such courses can be of a high professional standard and put over generic appraisal skills in a competent way, but what they cannot do is to cater for the unique characteristics of the organisation and the way appraisal operates there. They therefore tend to be seen as rather remote and lacking in relevance to the appraisers' context.

## Chapter 7

# Monitoring and maintenance

The chief personnel executive of an organisation employing more than 50,000 people and which had introduced comprehensive performance management and appraisal policies, when asked what he would do differently if he were to start again, replied that he would lay more emphasis on the importance of maintaining them. He was putting his finger on one of the eternal problems of appraisal – how to keep it alive and well. Great effort is often expended on setting it up in the first place, with very little thought given to the follow-through action needed once it is up and running. Yet the frequency with which organisations encounter difficulties with their appraisal schemes should give ample warning of how essential it is to monitor them from the outset, and to modify and correct any deficiencies at the earliest possible stage. If problems do arise, they have to be caught quickly, or the whole appraisal scheme rapidly generates scepticism and disillusionment that is hard to dispel – and which can make any effort to modify the scheme an uphill struggle.

Most of what is said in this chapter implies a central role for the personnel or HR department, despite the emphasis elsewhere in the book on moving away from monolithic, centrally driven appraisal schemes. It is certainly desirable, as ever, to evaluate appraisal in a manner that involves line management and others. But the complexities of the exercise and the need, in many respects, for a broader perspective indicates that this is an area where personnel have to act as the driving force and prime facilitators.

## Performance Indicators for Performance Appraisal

How do we recognise excellence in an appraisal scheme? What are the criteria by which an appraisal scheme might be judged successful or unsuccessful? These can be broken down into short-term and long-term criteria, with the former being much easier to define than the latter.

### Short-term criteria

As far as monitoring the effectiveness of the appraisal scheme in its first year or so of operation is concerned, it is obviously the short-term criteria that are relevant. These include:

- *Completion rate.* The most basic measure of all is whether the appraisals are actually carried out. Research over the years has shown just how often appraisals are not done, and how far managers will go to avoid them. If the appraisal scheme has been well-designed, with a good level of consultation, this should not happen. Where all appraisal forms go to central personnel, it is relatively easy to check on completion. Contemporary trends in appraisal, however, mean that it is less often the case that personnel are automatically sent copies of appraisal documents. They tend to reside with the appraisee and appraiser as working documents to be referred to when, say, objectives are subject to interim review or development needs are discussed. There is a lot to be said for this practice, as it makes appraisal reports live documents rather than just file fodder. But it need not preclude the sending of a simple action sheet to the personnel division indicating what action recommendations, if any, have been agreed. This can serve the triple function of notifying personnel that the appraisal has been done, informing them if there are some action recommendations that fall within their sphere of responsibility, and providing them with a means of checking on the subsequent implementation of action recommendations.

    There will always be a few appraisals that are not done for one good reason or another, but any sizeable short-fall should set alarm bells ringing. The MD of one business services organisation decided to give a further encouragement to the prompt and full completion of appraisals; he made it a pre-condition for considering promotion applications from the appraisers.

- *Action generated.* Another useful indicator of how things are going is the extent and type of action recommendations generated by the appraisal. If appraisal documents produce few agreed action points, then something is not quite right, the more so if there is any indication of development needs – how are they going to be dealt with? The nature of the action recommended is as important as the quantity. If the bulk of the action is to be taken outside the immediate job context – such as external training courses – then it may be an indication that the appraiser and appraisee are not looking hard enough at what they can do together to improve performance. Indeed, if most of the recommendations coming forward relate just to appraisers or to appraisees, the question needs to be asked as to whether the system is working as intended. It is reasonable for the majority of action following appraisals to be for implementation by the appraisees (overall, that is – clearly there will be individual cases where this is not so), but not all of it. If appraisers are taking responsibility for nearly all the post-appraisal action, then the suspicion arises that they are not getting their appraisees sufficiently involved in the process.

- *Quality of written reports.* Where the appraisal scheme entails the completion of a formal written report, the content of this can give some indication of how the process is operating. At its simplest, the issue is whether the report is being completed in the manner required. More searchingly, the written content can be evaluated in terms of how much is recorded, whether there are any inconsistencies or deficiencies (e.g. weaknesses being identified but no remedial action mentioned), and the frequency and nature of the dissenting comments recorded by appraisees. The general tone of the comments can reveal a great deal. For example, I can recall an appraisal report written after the appraisal interview by a senior civil servant which said: 'I would not like to see Jones at a promotion interview on this showing'. It was not hard to imagine that the appraisal session had been conducted in a rather gruelling fashion, more akin to a promotion interview than an appraisal interview. Analysing all written reports, especially in a systematic way, is usually far too time-consuming to be worthwhile. It is more realistic to do it on a sampling basis, or to rely on the corrective input from other appraisers where more than one manager is involved (e.g. where the appraisal is done by the appraisee's immediate boss but also seen by the boss two levels up) –

though in the latter case, this function needs to be emphasised in training as part of the second appraiser's role.

- *Attitudes and the perceived value of appraisal.* From action to reaction – how appraisers and appraisees feel about the scheme once they have been through a round of appraisals, what they see as the benefits and outcomes, what they see as the problems, are all important indicators of how the scheme is working. Depending on when they are collected, these reactions can be short or long-term criteria. If the participants feel positive about the scheme and see it as leading to useful developments (e.g. performance improvement, knowing where they stand, greater role clarity), then there is some cause for optimism. Although these might be subjective responses, they are as important as any hard data; the commitment of the participants rests on them. Any reported difficulties in the way the appraisals were conducted (too much emphasis on objectives, insufficient recognition of work done well, avoidance of giving feedback on the part of appraisers, and so on) from the perspective of either appraisers or appraisees, can be investigated and remedial action taken.

- *Equity.* The concept of equity in relation to monitoring performance appraisal has two main aspects. One is the way reward decisions are made and the spread of assessments that give rise to them. Do certain sections of the organisation fare significantly better than others in terms of assessments and rewards, and if so is it justifiable – are they really better? The other aspect concerns equal opportunities and unfair discrimination. Are the distributions of assessments, and the content of appraisals generally, similar for both sexes and across ethnic groups? Inequity in either of these domains is likely to pose severe problems, not least in the area of law, for the organisation and its appraisal scheme. Appraisals have not only to be fair, they have to be seen to be fair.

### Long-term criteria

It could be argued that there should not be any long-term criteria for the effectiveness of an appraisal scheme, because no scheme should continue in the same form for a long period if it is to remain relevant to the changing circumstances of the organisation. But given that there is likely to be some continuity in the appraisal arrangements — most changes in appraisal schemes are more in the nature of evolution than revolution — it does seem reasonable to look at the longer-term benefits the appraisal and related processes have produced. In fact, it is probably worth considering what the long-term criteria might be even if there is no intention to actually try to measure them. The rationale for this is simply that it often clarifies the organisation's thinking about appraisal to formally identify what the long-term success of an appraisal scheme might look like. It is, of course, possible that such a process will bring to light the fact that the organisation sees appraisal as an activity that has only short-term pay-offs. For those — hopefully the majority — who do see appraisal as having a strategic contribution to make, four broad criteria that might guide their evaluation are outlined below. None of them are determined solely by the effectiveness of appraisal, but in each case the appraisal scheme has a role to play and can reasonably be assessed in that context.

- *Organisational performance.* There are obviously many factors that influence the basic indices of organisational performance, and some of them (such as government policy or the state of the economy in general) are more potent in their effect than appraisal can ever be. None the less, appraisal policies — particularly within a performance management framework — should have some effect. Perhaps the clearest indicator of their impact on organisational performance in the broadest sense is the extent to which the targets set for individuals are seen as being achieved. If they are, and if those targets relate in a systematic way to the business plan, then the appraisal process might fairly be judged to be making an effective contribution.
- *Quality of staff.* One of the main functions of appraisal is, or should be, the development of staff. If it is successful in that, then the organisation will find either that it has enough trained employees to meet its normal requirements at any given time, or that it can readily identify where gaps are likely to occur (which might arise through problems in recruitment) and take remedial action. In other words, one of the criteria that can be used is whether the promotion vacancies or new posts can be filled from within the organisation by staff of acceptable quality.
- *Retention of staff.* Appraisal is a communication device, and in

the process of discussing performance and meeting development needs, problems that might cause individuals to leave the organisation can be detected and (sometimes) dealt with. If the appraisal scheme is an effective vehicle for motivating people and raising job involvement and job satisfaction, it can help to minimise the wastage rate and boost staff retention, so saving the money that might otherwise be used in recruiting and training new staff.

• *Levels of commitment.* As implied by the last point, an effective appraisal system should eventually – not overnight – lead to more positive attitudes to the job and to the organisation. Thus, levels of job involvement, job satisfaction and organisational commitment are all indicators that are relevant to judging how well an appraisal system is operating and the kind of impact it is making in the long term (measurement of commitment will be discussed shortly).

## Methods and Sources of Evaluation

To say what the evaluation criteria might be is one thing, but how to actually collect the data is quite another. The methods of evaluation are implicit in most of the criteria outlined above, however, more needs to be said about evaluating three of them: attitudes and perceived value, equity, and levels of commitment.

### Measuring attitudes to appraisal and its perceived value

There are two main methods available here, the interview and the questionnaire, and both can be targeted on appraisers and appraisees alike. Interviews produce richer data – the interviewers can ask probing questions and follow up on interesting observations, and will be able to grasp the nuances of the appraisal process and its context for the people they are interviewing. The three drawbacks of this approach are: (a) it is time consuming, and this inevitably limits the sample size; (b) it is sometimes difficult to analyse and summarise this kind of qualitative data; and (c) it does not give the respondents anonymity, which may inhibit their frankness. The pros and cons of the questionnaire method are just the opposite. On the positive side, it allows for larger samples, quantitative analysis, and can afford anonymity to the respondents. The cost of this is that it does not yield the richness and detail of observations that come from interviews. Also, not all organisations have the resources or expertise to run questionnaire surveys, or can afford to commission them from outside consultants (a cheaper alternative to the latter is to approach an occupational psychology department or a business school in a university and ask if any students would care to run an evaluation study as a project – the disadvantage here being that the company loses some control over the evaluation process).

The core content of the evaluation is much the same whichever method is used. The areas to be covered are likely to be:

- background details of the respondent (age, sex, job)
- what was discussed in the appraisal
- perceptions of the effectiveness and outcomes
- overall attitudes to the appraisal scheme.

The exact content and framing of questions will depend on the nature of the appraisal system and the level of the respondents. Appendix C gives examples of general questionnaire items that might also be used as core questions in an interview (to be followed up with subsidiary questions as appropriate). As most organisations have a lot more experience of interviewing than of mounting questionnaire surveys, the basic steps involved in the latter are described in Box 7.1.

---

**Box 7.1: Running a questionnaire-based evaluation study**

It is not as difficult to run questionnaire surveys as might be imagined; most medium or large organisations should be able to cope with them (for extra guidance see Walters, 1990). The sequence to follow is this:

1. The aim of the survey and when it is to be carried out are the first things to consider, as the two questions are linked. If the chief objective is to find out what went on in the interview and whether the appraisers followed the training guidelines they had been given, then the survey has to be done as soon as possible

after the interviews have taken place (otherwise, people simply forget and do not report accurately). If, on the other hand, the main concern is the effects and outcomes of the appraisal process, then the questionnaires have to go out long enough after the appraisal for some effects to have been observed – perhaps 3 – 6 months at least. Ideally, both types of information are sought. This means either having two separate surveys or staggering the distribution of the questionnaires, some going out immediately after the appraisals and some rather later. The latter is probably the more economical approach, but care has to be taken that the time elapsed since the appraisal is taken account of in analysing the data and interpreting the findings.

2. Decide on the sample. To a large extent this depends on the size of the organisation and the resources available. In small companies, it should be possible to cover all appraisees and appraisers (though a decision has to be taken about whether staff who find themselves in both roles are to be burdened with completing two questionnaires, one as appraisee and one as appraiser). In larger organisations, some kind of sampling will probably be necessary. The sampling can be done on a random basis from personnel records, or various divisions can be chosen and all staff in them covered. The main thing is to ensure that the sample is (a) as representative as possible in terms of age, sex, level, function and geographical area, and (b) large enough to give worthwhile information – it is important to remember that the response rate may be as low as 50 per cent, though hopefully it will be more like 75 per cent.

3. Develop a pool of questions on the basis of what you want to ask about the appraisals and what effects they have had. One set of items will be for appraisers, and the other set – on a separate questionnaire – will be for appraisees. See Appendix C for some suggestions. Keep in mind the length of the questionnaire and the time it takes to complete; most people will not spent more than around 20 minutes on it.

4. Put the items together in questionnaire format, paying particular attention to the instructions (on how to complete the questionnaire) and the wording of the items. In the case of the instructions, are they clear and appropriate to the kind of response format (e.g. ticking one of a series of response alternatives)? And in relation to the item wording, avoid asking two questions in one, e.g. 'Did the appraisal lead to an increase in your job satisfaction and performance?' (whatever the answer, you will not know if the respondent was referring to

satisfaction, performance, or both). If the intention is to record and analyse the questionnaire data by computer, then this will need to be reflected in the questionnaire format (as illustrated in Appendix C).

5. Pilot the draft questionnaires by giving them to a small group of staff at the target levels. When they have completed them, discuss the content and format of the questionnaire with the pilot sample. Were the instructions and the questions clear? Was any item especially difficult to answer or posed problems in some way? Was anything omitted that they felt was important? Did they have a common understanding of what the items meant? How long did it take to complete?

6. Redraft the questionnaire in the light of this feedback, and send it out to the designated sample with a suitable covering letter. The latter should:
− make clear the purpose of the exercise
− say who will receive the output from it and how it will be used
− if possible, guarantee anonymity for the respondent
− state who has authorised the evaluation study
− explain how the sample has been chosen
− ask for the cooperation of the person receiving the questionnaire and give an indication of the (short) time it takes to answer it
− indicate where to send it on completion.

7. In the case of large samples, the data can be analysed using any one of a variety of statistical packages available (e.g. SPSS). For smaller sample sizes, it is possible to do the analysis manually. Often, simple percentage response breakdowns on each question will provide the information necessary, though further analysis using simple statistics like chi-squared will help bring out any significant differences between the various staff groups (i.e. analysing the data by sex, function, level and so on).

In any evaluation study aimed at investigating attitudes and perceptions, whether by interview or questionnaire, the quality of the information obtained will, in part, depend on the degree to which the respondents cooperate. If members of trade unions or staff associations are involved, then these bodies should be consulted on the evaluation exercise and asked for their suggestions on its content. This will not only help to gain their support for the study, and so encourage their members to participate, but will also increase their interest in the findings and in implementing changes as a result of them. Senior management involvement and backing should be sought for the same reasons. After gaining all this support, employees can be informed of the impending study, told that it has been sanctioned by the various interested parties, and asked for their cooperation through the medium of in-house publications (newsletters etc.) or departmental meetings.

When it comes to interpreting evaluation data of this kind, a number of issues arise. It has to be recognised that the observations collected are subjective, although they represent the reality for the people concerned and will determine their reactions to the appraisal process. But there will be some inconsistencies, not least between appraisers and appraisees. Research (Sofer and Tuchman, 1970) has shown how the two parties often recall the actual content of the interview rather differently. The objective truth, such as it is, usually lies somewhere between the two.

More difficult is to ascertain what constitutes a satisfactory set of results. For example, is it good to have 30 per cent of appraisees feeling that the appraisal helped improve their performance, or is that rather low? Can we realistically expect a 100 per cent positive response? The best way to answer questions of this kind is to have some 'norms' − a picture of what average results look like − so that the organisation can compare their results against them and see if they were higher, lower or the same. The nearest available thing to norms of this kind is given by Fletcher and Williams (1992, pages 87 − 89), who present some of the findings from seven studies in public and private sectors, covering 5,940 appraisees and 1,332 appraisers.

Once the results are in and have been analysed, their implications for the way the appraisal scheme is operating and how it might be modified have to be considered. The general principle of encouraging ownership and participation in appraisal can be followed through here, by arranging group feedback sessions in which small groups of appraisers (and possibly, in separate sessions, appraisees) are presented with the main findings of the evaluation and invited to discuss them and their implications. This both provides feedback and acts as a vehicle for generating improvement. If problems in the way the appraisal scheme is running have been identified, some action has to be taken − there is not much point doing the evaluation if the will to act on the findings is lacking. This may entail additional training (possibly targeted at certain groups or particular skills), clarification of the written guidance, or changes to the nature of the scheme itself. Most important is that something should be seen to be done, and done quickly.

## Assessing equity: the fairness of the distribution

The basic task here is to collect all the relevant data from the appraisal documentation and recommendations. This is usually done by the central personnel department, monitoring the distributions of ratings and pay recommendations and checking to see that there are no unjustifiable variations between staff groups (e.g. Williams and Walker, 1985). The relevant information, and the desire to collect it, has to be there of course. I well remember asking the personnel manager responsible for appraisal in a major manufacturing company whether they did any ethnic monitoring of appraisal data, and getting the reply, 'No, I'm glad to say'. Given that any appraisal feeding into pay and promotion decisions can be the subject of legal challenge, his seems to be a dangerously short-sighted outlook.

It may be that the differences in the distribution of assessments are entirely justifiable. However, if a group of workers from a particular ethnic background do less well on performance ratings than do the majority of appraisees, the question is whether this genuinely reflects attributes of the appraisees or whether it is due to biased perceptions on the part of the appraisers. If there is evidence that this group of appraisees have less experience or lower educational levels, this could be the reason for the lower performance levels. On the other hand, if no such differences between them and the rest are observable, and no development action for them (or less than for the majority) was recommended by the appraisers, there would be cause for suspicion and concern.

A frequently encountered instance of where justifiable inequities can arise is in reward decisions. It is probably unrealistic to assume that all parts of the organisation are performing effectively, and this will be represented in the PRP recommendations. The problem is one of determining whether the higher levels of PRP awards being put forward by managers do reflect superior performance or just excessive leniency in assessment. As suggested in Chapter 3, the best way of sorting this out is to leave it to the line managers themselves to justify their pay recommendations to their peers, with personnel providing any statistical information that is relevant (e.g. changes in divisional output, expenditure, and so on over the year).

Whilst variations in appraisal data may be a function of sex, race, division etc. and have to be investigated, there is a broader level of evaluation and monitoring that needs to be done. This is checking to see if the *overall* distributions of ratings and merit pay increases look right, which implies that there is some idea at the outset of what they should be. This is clearly essential if pay costs − and employee career expectations − are to be kept under control. The case of a major UK bank illustrates this. It started out with the expectation that 10−15 per cent of staff would be assessed as having exceeded their targets, 60−70 per cent as having met their targets, and 10−20 per cent as having fallen short of target. They did not get quite this kind of distribution, as the actual proportion of staff in each category was 22 per cent, 69 per cent and 9 per cent. This is not far off what they wanted, but the impact on the pay bill is worth pointing up. The top group, which contained 7−12 per cent more staff than anticipated, got a 10 per cent bonus, while the bottom group, which had 1−10 per cent fewer staff in it than anticipated got a 2.5 per cent bonus. If the distribution had departed much further from what was expected and desired, the consequences could have been fairly serious.

Sometimes the overall distribution produces quite a different problem. The overall performance rating for 6,000 middle range administrative staff in a large county council after one year of a new appraisal and PRP scheme looked like this (Fletcher and Williams in IPM, 1992):

| Highest Rating | 1 | 2 | 3 | 4 | 5 | Lowest Rating |
|---|---|---|---|---|---|---|
| % Staff | .01 | 5.2 | 93.1 | 1.0 | .01 | |

The problem here is one of almost everyone being rated in the middle. Given that the rating is a basis for PRP decisions, this is very unhelpful as it fails to discriminate effectively between differing performance levels (unless one makes the unlikely assumption that there were virtually no differences amongst 6,000 staff). The fact that PRP was new in this organisation may have contributed to the excessive caution of the appraisers. In cases of this kind, those who have responsibility for appraisal within the organisation have to take some corrective action. Again, the best way to do this is by group feedback sessions backed up by written guidance.

The general point then, is that it is helpful (essential in the case of PRP systems) to have some idea of what the rating distributions should be overall, and to communicate this to the appraisers — and probably to the appraisees (as a restraint on expectations). Monitoring appraisal assessments, and checking to see if there are unexplained variations in them, is a key part of the evaluation process. Neglecting to do so can cost the organisation dear in more ways than one.

## Measuring levels of commitment

If introducing or revising performance appraisal is a significant organisational development intervention, then it should have broader and longer-term effects on communication, staff attitudes to the organisation and their levels of involvement in their work. All these and more can be tapped by a questionnaire survey, but there is a basic problem. To be meaningful as an evaluation of the changes brought about by appraisal, or any other intervention, there has to be a base-line measure against which to project those changes. In other words, you need a before-and-after measurement strategy. An example of this is given in Box 7.2.

---

**Box 7.2: A long-term evaluation of appraisal impact in HMSO\***

The first stage of this evaluation exercise was carried out in Her Majesty's Stationery Office before appraisal was instituted, and consisted of a questionnaire covering general attitudes to work, supervision and communications with management. It was sent to 500 staff at levels ranging from clerical to middle management. Three years later, some of the same questions were included in another questionnaire, in which the rest (the majority) of the items focused on the appraisal interviews that had taken place in the intervening period. The sample, matched with the previous one, was against 500 staff, and again a high response rate was achieved.

---

Comparison of the two sets of data showed that there had been some significant improvements. Higher levels of communication and more frequent job discussions were reported between subordinates and both their immediate bosses and their bosses two levels up (both these levels were involved in the appraisal process). They reported themselves as feeling much freer to talk to their managers than they did before. These findings reflected one of the fundamental, longer-term aims of appraisal in the organisation – greater subordinate – manager contact and dialogue. Were they only attributable to the introduction of appraisal? It is difficult to say, though it would be extremely unlikely that appraisal had not played a major part. One further piece of validating evidence is that both surveys included 'dummy' items that were not related to the anticipated impact of the appraisal and which were not expected to show changes; these items did indeed show no change.

*(Dulewicz *et al.*, 1976; Fletcher and Williams, 1992)

Rather than constructing questionnaires from scratch, as in the HMSO example, an alternative is to use one or more of the standard measures of job satisfaction, organisational commitment and similar variables. This saves time and effort and, more importantly, has the advantage of offering the opportunity to compare the organisation's scores on these measures with those published from other organisations. This makes it possible to look at the changes that have taken place within the organisation *and* at whether the levels of job satisfaction etc. are higher or lower than elsewhere. Research (Fletcher and Williams in IPM, 1992) on performance management using this approach demonstrated how the differing quality of performance management schemes was reflected in the scores on such variables. Acquiring these kinds of measures is not very difficult. They are readily available in the occupational psychology literature and can, in most cases, be used without having to purchase them. A good general source is Cook *et al.* (1981). Some specific measures that are relevant and the references for them are listed in Appendix D. It may be wise to get some guidance from a Chartered Occupational Psychologist if the organisation is contemplating incorporating measures of this type in its long-term evaluation of appraisal.

## In Conclusion

It is not easy to carry out evaluation exercises, and I have often been struck by the contrast between organisations' willingness to commit considerable human and financial resources to setting up personnel systems – be they psychometric tests in selection, assessment centres, appraisal schemes or whatever – and their extreme reluctance to commit a fraction of those resources to seeing if they were getting their money's worth. It may be the difficulty of doing evaluation work, it may be that the organisation does not think it has the expertise, but I have a terrible feeling that, in quite a few cases, it comes down to not wanting to know. Some managers responsible for designing systems have an understandable resistance to finding that what they have done is not actually working very well, with all the implications that has for their self-esteem, their standing with the organisation and the subsequent effort they have to put in to get things right. Small wonder that they show little enthusiasm for evaluation, with the risks that it may carry for them personally. To overcome this, it needs to be publicly recognised from the outset (the design stage) – by everyone involved – that it is the exception rather than the rule for appraisal schemes to run perfectly from day one, and that evaluation and further improvement is a normal expectation.

# Chapter 8

# Appraising – and developing – potential

Much of the content of the previous chapters has focused on the appraisal of performance, albeit with an eye to motivating and developing individuals over the review period. Traditionally, however, appraisal has a longer-term perspective in contributing to the assessment and development of potential. For a long time, the appraisal of performance and promotability and/or long-term potential were both parts of the same exercise and recorded on the same form – and indeed still are in a good number of organisations. The problems of linking the discussion of current performance with rewards, which include promotion, led to many appraisal schemes separating the two functions out. As a result, it has become common for the appraisal of potential to be carried out at a different time of the year and to be written on different report forms from the appraisal of on-going performance. This assessment, in contrast to the appraisal of performance, is often not disclosed.

The economic pressures of the early 1980s seem to have caused something of a rethink on this aspect of appraisal. The survey by Long (1986) showed that the proportion of organisations listing the assessment of promotability and potential as one of the main purposes of appraisal had fallen appreciably, from 87 per cent to 71 per cent. Career planning was also less often seen as an important aspect of appraisal. The causes of this shift in emphasis are probably the uncertain economic outlook of the time, which made it harder to project ahead and to envisage growth with much confidence, and the fact that many organisations had shed labour in the previous five years and consequently had fewer promotion opportunities on offer. With the changes in organisations that have taken place in the last few years – not least the continued slim-lining and delayering – and the recession of the early 1990s, these problems have scarcely improved. In some ways, they have got worse. Not only are there fewer promotion opportunities as such, but given the rate of organisational change, when and where they occur is less predictable. The pattern of career progression is consequently less stable for many people, and less likely to be continued within the same organisation.

These circumstances, far from suggesting that promotability and potential should be taken off the appraisal agenda, indicate that the career progression of the individual needs to be addressed with much greater care. If there are fewer promotions to be had, then it is even more essential that the process of deciding who will get them is seen to be fair and effective. If career development opportunities increasingly lie outside the organisation, then the latter cannot rely quite so much on the loyalty and company commitment of individual employees as a motivating force. Moreover, the nature of career development, either inside or outside the organisation, is changing. With flatter organisations and fewer senior positions, for many people development is going to involve sideways moves or job enlargement rather than a straight promotion. In effect, a new contract has to be instituted, whereby the organisation undertakes to assess individuals' potential and to help them develop – ultimately, if necessary, outside the organisation. As part of this, self-development needs to be encouraged; if organisations are less able to guarantee future opportunities, then individuals can be provided with the experiences and skills to become more autonomous in facilitating their own career progression. Returning to the theme of what has been said earlier in this book about the aims of appraisal, there has to be some balance between organisational and individual needs, and only by retaining the assessment and development of potential as part of the appraisal process (in the widest sense) can this be achieved. It may seem a trifle idealistic to suggest that organisations should assist their employees in developing themselves for possible career progression elsewhere, but in reality it is in the organisations' interests also. As pointed out above, they cannot rely on loyalty to the company in the way they did previously, nor can they know precisely who they will and who they will not need. The best strategy on all counts is to help people help themselves in this direction.

Deciding the best methods for assessing and developing potential is not at all straightforward, however. One obvious basis to work from is present performance, as reflected in appraisal and other data. But the reason for having an assessment of potential is precisely because present performance is by no means a completely reliable indicator of future performance. It is certainly true in nearly all cases that if an individual is not performing well at the existing level, they are very unlikely to do better at more senior levels, and will probably be even worse. The question is, which of the majority of staff who are performing satisfactorily in their current jobs have the latent ability and aptitude to progress further and to be successful one or more levels higher in the organisation? How are those latent abilities and aptitudes to be assessed? The main methods for doing this are described and evaluated below. Before looking at them, though, there is another broad issue to consider: what is it, from the organisation's viewpoint, that people are being assessed and developed for?

One way of explaining this is to give an example from my own experience. I was approached by the newly appointed personnel director of a large company, who was seeking assistance in implementing a psychometrically based assessment and development programme for all middle and senior managers in the company – a big project given the numbers involved. The aim was to assess the managers' potential and to find some way of developing them. All very worthy, but developing them for what, I asked? Potential for what? Essentially, the answer took the form: 'Because it's a good thing, isn't it?' It rapidly became evident that (a) there was no idea of what abilities or competencies were needed to be effective at senior levels within the organisation, (b) there was no willingness to try to find out what these might be, (c) there was no idea about where the company was going in the next few years, the implications for the kinds of skills and attributes they would then need in their managers, and how this would inform development efforts now, and (d) there were insufficient resources to handle the development activity that would follow from such a large-scale assessment process.

Although more career development than before will lead to movement between organisations rather than simply within them, it remains important for organisations to try to identify what their needs are likely to be. If they do not, then there is a good chance that they will end up with the wrong mix of abilities and competencies for the situation they find themselves in a few years down the line. Techniques for analysing their requirements are largely those discussed in relation to competency-based appraisal in Chapter 3. However, they will also be mentioned again below in relation to some of the methods of appraising potential, specifically those that are focused on longer-term potential rather than short-term promotability.

## The Conventional Appraisal Process as a Means of Assessing Potential

The main role for appraisal in the context of career development is as an opportunity to discuss short-term training and development needs and for the appraisee to talk over career aspirations with the appraiser. But the conventional appraisal process has been found severely wanting as a means of assessing long-term potential, though it does have a more worthwhile contribution to make to immediate promotion decisions. The problems of using performance appraisal in this context are numerous:

- As a means of assessing current performance – which is the basis of the promotion/potential judgment – its accuracy leaves a lot to be desired.
- The direct linking of promotion or other rewards to the performance discussion has detrimental effects on the latter.
- Managers are sometimes reluctant to lose their best people, and it is not unknown for this to affect their written assessments of potential.
- The manager's own style may inhibit the opportunity for a subordinate to demonstrate potential.
- Where judgments about long-term potential for senior management levels are needed, line managers are not necessarily the best people to comment, as they may not have reached that level themselves and therefore not possess first-hand experience of what is required.
- The limited breadth of perspective of individual managers can mean that they are unaware of the performance standards required for promotion and of the range of opportunities available – which may give rise to the creation of false (unduly high or low) expectations in the appraisee.

Several of these problems (and particularly the last one) are accentuated in appraisal schemes that are highly devolved and line-owned, which suggests that in such circumstances it is especially unwise to let the assessment of potential rest solely on the appraisal process. However, even in centrally driven appraisal schemes, given all the other demands and burdens placed on the annual appraisal, it does not seem very sensible to add this one. Perhaps the best contribution the annual appraisal can make is as a short-listing mechanism: if appraisees are consistently performing at a high level (and perhaps have demonstrated this with more than one boss), then they are worth considering for promotion by whatever other review or assessment method is used. This way, the line manager still has a direct influence on promotion decisions, but not the deciding one.

## Career Review Panels

One of the most common methods of making assessments about potential and feeding them into career planning is through the use of career review panels (CRPs) (also known by a variety of other, similar names). CRPs usually consist of a panel of senior managers, convened by the personnel department, who periodically review either all managers at a specific level, or on a selective basis. Their task is to make some assessment of the promotability of individuals and to draw up a career plan for them. In doing this, they will have access to appraisal forms and possibly to additional reports made by appraisers specifically for this purpose. They may also interview staff if they feel this would be helpful. Throughout their deliberations, they have input from personnel, which should help inform them of the range of opportunities available, the people who might fill them, and the manpower planning situation in the short and medium term.

The advantages of this approach are that it is flexible, it provides a wider perspective than can be achieved by any one appraiser, it still involves line management, it has credibility because of the senior level of the people on the panel and it does not interfere with the normal appraisal process. The limitations of CRPs is that they remain largely dependent on the input from the performance appraisal to assess potential (though that input might relate to a broader time span and the appraisee's performance under more than one appraiser). They are still in the position of trying to judge potential on the basis of present performance. Also, some or all members of the panel may have little or no direct contact with the people whose potential they are trying to assess. Looking at the pros and cons of CRPs overall, whilst they are helpful in making decisions on short-term promotions, the method seems to have most to offer where it is used as a career planning mechanism based on assessments of potential done by other means.

## The Interview in Assessing Potential

The interview still seems to be the most popular way of deciding suitability for promotion to a specific post. The form of the interview may vary, from a one-to-one interview with the manager who has a vacancy to fill, to a panel interview where personnel and other departments are represented. How candidates are chosen to attend for the interview can be based on personal applications to the manager concerned, on appraisal data, and on psychometric test results. Leaving the last-mentioned of these aside for the moment (it will be dealt with in depth below), the use of the interview usually takes a fairly conventional form. Typically, questions centre on:

- the individual's career so far, and the reasons for the decisions they have taken
- the attraction of the position they are applying for and how they would tackle it
- the way they perceive the fit between their experience and abilities and the position they are applying for
- future career aspirations and direction
- various hypothetical questions of the 'what would you do if' and 'how would you do such-and-such' variety.

The advantages of interviews are that they are fairly easy to arrange, and that they are usually considered to be an essential part of the promotion process, if only so that the manager with the vacancy to fill can have a say in who is appointed, and the candidates can meet the person they would be working with. Alas, all that might be said of interviews in general applies to them in this context too. The typical, unstructured interview by the untrained interviewer remains an abysmal selection tool, for the many reasons that the research spanning three-quarters of a century has demonstrated. The outcome is as likely to be determined by the biases of the interviewers and what they have failed to find out as by anything more positive. Happily, this does not mean that the interview is devoid of value in contributing to the assessment of potential, as more recent developments in interview techniques show.

## Behaviourally-based interview methods

It has long been known that more structured approaches to interviewing increase its effectiveness. There are now a number of behaviourally based interviewing techniques that are applicable in assessing promotability and potential and have been shown to be valid – in other words, they predict performance with some success (Harris, 1989; Eder and Ferris, 1989). One example, the situational interview, is described in Box 8.1. This is quite a sophisticated technique, but there are alternatives that, although simpler, are still very useful. If the competencies or dimensions relevant to effective performance in the post are known, then it is possible to develop a structured interview around them. Thus, if it is known that organisation and planning are key elements in the job, then a series of questions on this theme can be drawn up to assess the extent to which the candidate has demonstrated a capacity for planning and organisation. Examples might be: 'Tell us about how you establish the priorities in your present job'; 'Describe how you go about planning and organising your own work and time'; 'What was the most difficult planning task you have had? Tell us about it', and so on. Questions of this kind yield useful information and are targeted on the important aspects of the job, and they do deal with actual rather than anticipated behaviour. But they all relate to what the individual has done in the past, at a lower level, with the limitations that implies. One of the strengths of the situational interview is that it seeks to project the candidate forward into their anticipated behaviour in the role they are being assessed for. It is true that just because someone says they will act in a particular way, it is not necessarily the case that they will do so in reality. However, the evidence for the validity of the situational interview is some reassurance here (Latham and Saari, 1984). Apart from anything else, at least the situational interview tells you whether the candidates *know* what the right answer is, irrespective of whether they will really act that way.

---

**Box 8.1  The situational interview\***

This novel approach to interviewing requires the organisation first to carry out, or have access to, a critical incidents job analysis of the position to be filled (see pages 14–15). The incidents identified will describe various situations and problems that typically arise in the job. The steps in constructing the situational interview are then as follows:

- A group of managers familiar with the job and level at which the vacancy or vacancies exist select a number of incidents that they agree on as being characteristic of the job and as sampling the main attributes necessary to perform effectively in it. So, for example, they may choose a reported incident where a manager had a problem with a subordinate because of a complaint about sexual harassment from another member of staff. The manager concerned passed it on to personnel to handle rather than deal with it personally.
- These incidents are turned into questions. In the case of the example given, it might be: 'One of your subordinates comes to you with a complaint about sexual harassment from another of your subordinates. You suspect it is true, though you have no other evidence to go on. What would you do in this situation?'
- The group of managers would then be asked to say, independently and on the basis of their knowledge of staff of varying standards at this level, how good, mediocre and poor performers would deal with the situation outlined. When they have done this, they discuss their answers to check that there is a good level of agreement in each case. In the example used here, they might come up with a set of benchmark answers like this:

    *Good performers*: try to deal with the situation themselves, but gather further information from the parties involved before coming to a judgment about what action is appropriate.

*Mediocre performer*: passes the matter on immediately to personnel without any attempt to gain further information or taking any responsibility for it.

*Poor performer*: calls in the party alleged to be doing the harassing and issues a stern warning without seeking further information and without giving them an opportunity to answer the allegation.

- Answers reflecting these three strategies might be scored 1, 3, and 5 respectively. A complete set of questions and graded answers is arrived at through the same process, in such a way that all the key dimensions of the job are covered. The example used here might reflect both judgment and supervisory ability.
- The interview takes place and candidates are posed the questions. Their answers are taken down by one of the interviewers (the method requires a panel of at least two).
- Candidates' answers are scored, preferably independently by two or more raters, in terms of how they relate to the benchmark answers. The raters then discuss their marks and come to an agreed assessment.

This approach to interviewing sounds just like presenting a set of hypothetical questions, and it is – but with some crucial differences. It is based on job analysis, the questions are chosen to cover the important performance dimensions, and the answers are quantitatively rated on how they compare with good and poor performers in the job. It is certainly a more demanding form of interview in terms of time and managers' involvement, but it has been shown to be much superior to conventional forms of interviewing in terms of its predictive power (Harris, 1989) – so at least it is time well spent. Also, it probably sounds more daunting to construct than it actually is.

*Latham *et al*. (1980); Latham (1989).

Whatever the relative merits of the various approaches to behaviourally based interviewing, all such structured interviews are likely to be better at yielding accurate assessments than unstructured interviews (Wright *et al.*, 1989). Panel interviews also seem to be superior to one-to-one interviews in this respect (Wiesner and Cronshaw, 1989). Without the use of behaviourally based methods, the interview as a means of assessing potential is likely to be little more than an exercise in impression management (Fletcher, 1989).

## Using Psychometric Tests in Assessing Potential

Psychometric testing is a complex topic, the full scope of which is beyond this book – readers are referred to Toplis, Dulewicz and Fletcher (1991) for a fuller treatment of the subject. Any organisation willing to invest the money in either buying in external consultants or in getting their own staff trained in testing can make use of the methods described below. Companies producing tests offer good (but fairly costly) training, and it inevitably tends to focus on their own particular products. It is therefore advisable first to get some independent advice as to what, *if any*, are the most appropriate kinds of tests for the situation and whether it is going to be more cost-effective to get company staff trained or to have it done by an external agency. The IPM Code of Practice on Psychological Testing points out that best sources of that advice are Chartered *Occupational* Psychologists. The British Psychological Society publishes a directory of Chartered Occupational Psychologists, and you will be more appropriately guided by this than by any of the other lists or directories they publish.

How can tests assess potential?

The huge growth in the use of psychometric tests over the last ten years or so, both here and elsewhere in Europe, has included an increase in their use to assess promotability and potential. What is the basis for thinking that psychometric tests can contribute to the assessment of potential? There are two broad categories of tests that need to be looked at here: one covers cognitive (intellectual) abilities and the other deals with personality attributes – though, strictly speaking, the latter are not 'tests' as they do not involve right or wrong answers. The argument that cognitive tests have something to say about potential is the strongest, or at least the most straightforward. It goes something like this:

- In many administrative, managerial and professional roles, a good level of intellectual ability is needed to perform effectively.
- The higher individuals go within these roles, the greater the demands made on them, and the greater their ability needs to be to cope.
- We therefore need to know that any candidates for higher

responsibility levels have the intellectual potential to perform effectively, which can be assessed by comparing their cognitive abilities against those of people already successfully performing at such levels.

- Because they can show whether an individual matches up to the intellectual level associated with people already at higher levels, tests can also give some indication as to whether individuals who are performing well in their present job are actually at their ceiling or whether they have the intellectual resources to progress further.

The question might be asked as to whether educational qualifications might not serve the same purpose. They can, but not nearly so well. The advantage of tests is that they often show up intellectual potential that is not evident in academic achievements. There are all sorts of reasons for this, but essentially it comes down to the fact that educational qualifications reflect a great deal else besides intellectual ability – home background and opportunity, parental attitudes, motivation, adolescent problems and rate of maturity, quality of teaching, and so on. Not surprisingly, then, psychometric tests given to adults are very often found to be more predictive of job success than are educational qualifications.

It is a little more difficult to specify the role of personality measures in assessing potential. In terms of promotability to a particular job, the case is fairly straightforward. Here, the demands of the job and the person specification for it will suggest some personality attributes that are likely to be essential for effective performance and some that are likely to be counter-productive. A personality questionnaire may thus be useful in providing some data on these qualities. However, when the issue is one of longer-term potential to perform effectively some years in the future at a higher level and across a range of jobs, the requirement is much less clear-cut. It is less certain what personality attributes will be needed. If a competency analysis of the work at this level has been conducted, that will help and give some pointers as to what will and will not facilitate performance. Without this, there are only two alternatives to follow. One is to give personality measures to existing high performers at this level and see if any particular pattern emerges. The problem here is that any profile that emerges tells you about how things are now, not necessarily about how things should be or will be in the future. This can be illustrated by an example from my own experience.

I was asked to carry out individual, psychometrically based assessments on the board of directors of a medium-sized company that had just been acquired by a large engineering and electronics firm. The tests showed a remarkably consistent pattern: most of the directors were intellectually highly able, but operated in a style that seldom exploited their potential in this direction. They were all strongly task-oriented, extremely high in drive and energy, quick to react, disinclined to think strategically, individualistic and uncooperative. The one exception to this was the MD, who was intellectually less capable than his colleagues but was the only one of them who had some capacity for teamwork and was probably the only one who could get them to move in the same direction. It was not difficult to see how the nature of the work in that company and the tendency for people to be attracted to (and promote) individuals like themselves had brought about this group of directorial clones. The recipe had worked for some time, and the company had grown rapidly to become very successful. Unfortunately, when the market changed and competition increased, they did not seem to have had the resources within the board to respond to it; they all continued to charge ahead in the same way, without thinking through a new strategy. The point of this example is that if one took the personality pattern of the high performers in this organisation as the model for assessing the potential of more junior managers, the result would be pretty disastrous in a few years' time. It does not mean that there is no value in taking account of the personality pattern of senior managers (quite apart from anything else, it may say a lot about the organisation and how it is likely to function), but to be guided entirely by that would be a mistake. An analysis of future directions and needs has to be built in to the picture.

The other alternative for guiding the use of personality measures in assessing long-term potential is reasonable deduction (or informed guesswork!). It is probably going to be the case that some characteristics are *not* going to be helpful. People who are emotionally unstable, extremely low in drive, excessively aggressive, and so on are much less likely to make progress to the top. People who are flexible, dynamic, outgoing, emotionally stable, etc. are more likely to be effective and to perform at higher levels. However, there are obvious limitations to this kind of approach, and it will only be helpful with some of the more extreme cases. One final, general point about personality questionnaires. Over the last few years, there have been some isolated but well-publicised attacks on the value of such measures. It has now been convincingly shown that these attacks are spurious and can be dismissed (Jackson and Rothstein, 1993). Personality questionnaires can be very useful, though they are certainly not either straightforward or always effective to apply.

### The ways in which tests are used

There are a variety of ways in which tests are applied in assessing potential and promotability:

- They may be given to external candidates as part of a selection procedure, not only to assess suitability for the job vacancy but also to get some idea of the individual's potential beyond that.
- Internal candidates for a promotion vacancy may be given a battery of tests to assess their suitability for the promotion in question.
- Individuals may go through a testing session as part of a career assessment process that is not related to a specific promotion or job vacancy, but which has the assessment of potential as one of its aims.
- Tests are often included as an element of the assessment centre process, which will be discussed in a later section in this chapter.

Quite often the testing of candidates is done within the organisation by those appropriately trained. But at middle and senior levels, it is common practice to send the individuals to an outside consultant – usually a Chartered Occupational Psychologist – to conduct the assessment. Apart from the higher level of expertise offered by taking this (possibly expensive) route, the main reason for it is political. Middle and senior management candidates are less happy to be put through such a searching assessment process by someone who may be junior to them in the organisation. The form of these assessments typically includes a battery of cognitive ability tests – numerical, verbal, logical reasoning and (perhaps) creative thinking – and one or two personality measures, as well as an in-depth interview with the consultant. The result is a report to the company which covers various aspects of work performance, and (where appropriate) an assessment of their suitability for a particular promotion vacancy, based on a job description and person specification. If the aim of the assessment has been more general, the report will include an assessment of overall career potential and will review career alternatives against the background of the individual's strengths and weaknesses. Appendix E gives an example of a report based on psychometric testing and an interview, aimed at assessing potential and career development needs. There is almost invariably some kind of feedback session with the candidate, where the assessor goes over the findings and discusses them with the individual, who may also receive a copy of the report.

It is never suggested that tests are sufficient by themselves to assess potential. They should always be employed as an additional input to other sources of information, such as existing performance, career progress to date, and possibly an interview. Their results and implications have to be interpreted in the light of all this information. An example of this is the use of individual assessments by the computer company ICL, where candidates for promotion at senior levels in some parts of the company were externally assessed, and the reports then used by the panel interviewers as one of the sources of information on which to plan their interview; they could probe the issues raised and look at them in the context of the job requirements. In this particular company, the use of tests was a carefully integrated aspect of HR practice (Jones, 1990).

### The pros and cons of psychometric assessment of potential

Although psychometric testing has become so popular and accessible, it is far from easy to use this approach effectively. There are many traps for the unwary, not least the availability of poor-quality tests (often marketed with great vigour and professionalism) and the advice of consultants who have no real expertise to back it up. The money and the competence required to apply tests successfully are the main drawbacks. There is also the problem of the candidates' attitudes and beliefs about tests. It is quite understandable for an individual to ask 'Why on earth does the company want me to do these tests? I have been working here for six years – they should know enough about me now.' Unless the role of tests, how they are used and can contribute to the assessment process, is carefully explained, there is likely to be resistance to using them.

On the positive side, tests offer the advantages of:

- Objectivity: they are not dependent on the feelings and biases of the tester.
- Validity: the research shows that tests of intellectual ability and personality can predict future performance effectively.
- Flexibility: there is a very wide range of measures available and so many different kinds of jobs and levels can be catered for.
- They offer a source of information outside, and additional to, what is available from other sources.
- They may, if the organisation uses them over a period of time, facilitate a comparison between candidates and the characteristics of staff already in more senior positions.

No doubt all of these advantages have played a part in persuading a large number of companies to go in for the psychometric assessment of potential in recent years. If the result is better selection of candidates for higher-level posts, then the costs of testing pale into insignificance. But, as has been indicated several times in this section, the use of tests does not guarantee improved assessment and judgment. It is all too common to find poor-quality products and practice in this field (Fletcher, 1992).

## Assessment Centres

Assessment Centres (ACs) have been around for about half a century now, but rather like psychometric tests have only become popular in this country in the last ten years or so. They are currently used by 47 per cent of UK organisations employing 1,000 or more staff (Mabey, 1992). The term 'assessment centre' is used to describe the process whereby a team of assessors uses an integrated series of assessment techniques to assess a group of candidates. Those techniques typically include psychometric tests, interviews, peer ratings and simulation exercises. It is the last mentioned of these that constitute the core of the AC. They are meant to simulate or sample the kinds of work that an individual has to do at the level being selected for. These can include group problem-solving tasks, individual decision-making exercises (e.g. in-tray exercises), business games, and interview role plays. Again, as with psychometric testing, this is a topic worthy of a book in itself, and the reader can be directed to an excellent one by Woodruffe (1990). The discussion of ACs offered here will be limited to a general outline of their use in assessing and developing potential, examination of some of the main issues associated with this method, and an evaluation of its worth.

## Setting up and running ACs

As with so many aspects of appraisal, the first stage is to identify the key attributes for effective performance at the target level – the level in the organisation at which you are trying to assess the potential to perform successfully. This usually involves some kind of competency analysis of the kind discussed several times in this book. Once the necessary competencies or behavioural dimensions have been decided, it becomes possible to judge what kinds of exercises might be used to assess them. The usual practice is to aim to have at least two, and preferably more, AC assessment techniques contributing to the assessment of each dimension. This ensures that the behaviour in question is sampled on separate occasions on different kinds of task, and possibly by different assessors – so providing a basis for making reliable judgments. A grid of the kind illustrated in Figure 8.1 can be drawn up to show the relationship between exercises and dimensions.

---

**Figure 8.1: The dimension assessment method grid for an AC**

The example given below is taken from an assessment centre described by Fletcher and Dulewicz (1984). It lists the 13 assessment dimensions down the left with the eight exercises along the top. Some of the latter are broken up into different stages, as they are quite long and have different components. The totals on the right of the grid give the number of exercises

---

contributing ratings to each dimension, while the totals at the bottom of the grid present the number of dimensions assessed in each exercise.

| Dimensions | In-tray | Committee Pt I (Presentation) | Committee Pt II (Discussion) | Business decisions (1) | Business decisions (2 – 5) | Business decisions (6 – 8) | Presentation (Business Plan) | Letter writing | Total |
|---|---|---|---|---|---|---|---|---|---|
| 1. Analytical ability | * | | | * | * | | * | | 4 |
| 2. Helicopter ability | * | | * | | | | * | | 3 |
| 3. Administrative ability | * | | | * | * | | * | | 4 |
| 4. Business sense | * | | | * | * | * | * | | 5 |
| 5. Written communication | * | | | | | | | * | 2 |
| 6. Oral communication | | * | * | | | | | * | 3 |
| 7. Perceptive listening | | * | * | | | | | | 2 |
| 8. Vigour | * | | | * | * | | * | | 4 |
| 9. Emotional adjustment | | * | * | | * | | | * | 4 |
| 10. Social skill | | | * | | * | * | | * | 4 |
| 11. Ascendancy | | * | * | | * | * | * | | 5 |
| 12. Flexibility | | | * | | * | * | | | 3 |
| 13. Relations with subordinates | * | | * | | | | | * | 3 |
| Total | 7 | 3 | 9 | 5 | 7 | 6 | 6 | 3 | 46 |

The simulation exercises should represent the work at the target level as accurately as possible, and to this end managers already at that level should be involved in providing material for the exercises. It is possible to buy AC exercises off-the-shelf from various consultancies and test producers, but most organisations rightly want the content and nature of the exercises to reflect their own work and culture as closely as possible – which means constructing them from scratch, probably with some help from a consultant experienced in this field. Once the dimensions, exercises and other assessment methods are devised and decided on, a timetable for the AC event and administrative matters, such as where it is to be run, can be settled. Two other vital issues have to be confronted while all this is going on: who are to be the assessors and how are they to be trained; and how are the candidates to be nominated for the AC?

The assessors should largely be managers in the organisation who are working at the target level, so at least they know the work and demands associated with it at the present time. Their involvement has two other benefits: it ensures input and part-ownership of the AC process by the line, and it gives the AC a degree of credibility with senior line management as a result. Getting this line input is far from easy, as it requires a considerable time commitment from the managers concerned. They need to be trained, and then to be able to act as assessors on enough AC events (assuming that there are a series of them) to maintain a consistent standard. The importance of the training cannot be overstated; the value of the whole AC rests on it. The assessors should have the background and rationale of the method explained, gain some experience of doing some or all of the exercises themselves, and be given instruction in behavioural assessment. In particular, they need to become thoroughly familiar with the competencies or dimensions they are assessing, and what kind of behaviour is covered by each of them, so that they can correctly classify the candidates' behaviour when they see it.

Apart from the line manager assessors, there will usually be some personnel department representatives and possibly also one or more outside consultants. Including the latter is very desirable, for two reasons. First, where occupational psychologists are concerned (and they often feature in this role because of their expertise in devising ACs), reviews of the research evidence suggest that their success in predicting performance from ACs is greater than that achieved by line managers (Gaugler *et al.*, 1987). Secondly, even with all the sophistication of the AC method, there is still a danger of the assessors selecting people they see as being similar to themselves. In other words, the AC becomes a glorified cloning process. The presence of external assessors reduces the chance of that happening.

How the candidates for the AC are to be identified is never altogether straightforward. The basic options are:

- self-nomination
- nomination by the boss
- qualification through passing exams etc.

Nomination by the boss has the advantage of being based on current performance, but given the inadequacies of appraisal as an assessment mechanism, relying solely on this source may mean that some good candidates are missed. Self-nomination is the best in terms of scanning all possible candidates who might have potential and who could have been overlooked. However, this can also lead to some very unsuitable candidates putting themselves forward, with two unfortunate consequences: they waste the organisation's resources by taking places on ACs which are costly to run, and they may set themselves up for experiences of failure that could be very discouraging or even damaging to them. There is some virtue in the argument that says that where self-nomination is allowed, there should be a first-stage screening process involving psychometric tests. There are a few organisations where certain objective criteria, typically passing professional exams to some level, are used to determine who should attend ACs. Where there are such criteria and they are relevant to the assessment of potential, then nomination is much more clear-cut.

The normal ratio of candidates to assessors is 2:1 or 3:1, and the number of candidates attending any one AC is normally within the range of 5–15. The duration of the AC depends on the number of assessment techniques it contains, but is usually 1–3 days. The last day or part of it is devoted to the assessors' conference, where each candidate's performance is reviewed in turn; all the information is scrutinised, candidate by candidate; and final ratings on each dimension agreed. The candidate will be given an Overall

Assessment Rating (OAR) which generally boils down to a judgment that the individual has (a) high potential, (b) possibly has high potential, or (c) does not appear to have high potential at the moment. The first two of these lead to fast-track development status.

In due course, the outcome of the AC and observations on the candidates' performance in it will be conveyed to them in an individual feedback session. This is usually given by one of the assessors and/or a personnel representative, and the candidate's line manager may also be present – which is important if the latter is to assist the candidate in implementing any development plans. The implications of the AC for career progression will be thoroughly discussed and whatever action is needed put in hand.

## Issues in the use of ACs

Some of the practical problems in using ACs have already been mentioned. There are, however, a number of other issues that personnel practitioners need to be aware of:

- *Self-fulfilling prophecies.* There is some danger of letting ACs create crown princes and princesses. Once individuals have been identified as having potential, special attention and resources are lavished on them, so it may not be surprising if they do well. The expectation that they will be high performers can also influence perceptions of their actual performance. It is important, then, that such individuals are subject to particularly careful assessment to see that they are living up to their promise. Equally, the judgment in an AC that an individual does not have high potential must not be allowed to become the kiss of death, with no further interest or resources being directed to their career progression. This leads on to the next issue.
- *The feedback process.* The feedback given after ACs leaves a lot to be desired and tends to be one of the weakest features of how they are operated. The primary problem is that it comes too long after the event to capitalise on it. If the feedback is to be meaningful, it has to be given while the experience is still fresh in the participants' minds; a week or more after the event is far too long. Also, it has to be especially sensitively handled with individuals who have not done well in the AC. It has been found

that failure in an AC (one aimed at identifying managerial potential) reduced psychological well-being and some aspects of motivation at least six months after the event (Fletcher, 1991). There is sometimes a need for counselling on a longer-term basis, so that individuals do not feel that their career is somehow over and that they are no longer valued; not everyone can be a high-flyer.

- *Cost-effectiveness.* There is no doubt that ACs are the most expensive assessment process to run. It is impossible to give a precise cost per candidate, since the content and duration of ACs varies so much, as does the number of candidates put through them (obviously, the set-up costs as a proportion of total costs diminish with increasing numbers put through the AC). Utility analysis shows that the financial benefits of better selection using ACs far outweigh the expense of the method, see Woodruffe (1990, pages 28–31). This does not mean, though, that it is impossible to achieve nearly as good results through using cheaper methods. The main alternative to ACs is using psychometric tests, which are certainly cheaper and almost as predictive of future performance as are ACs. The debate about the relative cost-effectiveness of the two methods will go on and on, but in a sense there can never be an answer. The reason is that there is no way of financially evaluating either the superiority of the AC as a development tool or its face validity (the extent to which it *looks* as though it is measuring what it claims to) for both candidates and assessors. However, the experience of being trained as an assessor on an AC seems to improve a manager's assessment skills in other situations, such as performance appraisal – another valuable consequence of the method.

- *Preparing the candidates.* Because of its unique and demanding nature, the AC has the potential to throw some people a little off-balance. It is important to give candidates an idea of what to expect (the Civil Service Selection Board, for example, sends out a booklet describing in some detail what the candidates will be doing over the two days). It is also desirable to break them in gently, by having less demanding exercises, or 'unfreezing' exercises, first. Anxiety generated by the AC itself, which is not generally characteristic of the candidate, can adversely affect and distort performance at ACs (Fletcher and Kerslake, 1993), and assessors need to be aware of this.

- *The use of competencies/dimensions.* There is much academic debate about these, and whether ACs really measure them in the way they claim to. One thing is clear, however, and that is that the assessment dimensions used in ACs should not be too numerous. It has been shown that more dimensions does not mean more refined judgment — quite the opposite (Gaugler *et al.*, 1987). It is probably better to focus on a smaller number of essential competencies and to train assessors to rate them effectively than to go for long lists of 15 or more dimensions. Interestingly, research at Henley Management College (Dulewicz, 1989; Dulewicz and Herbert, 1992) has come up with 12 'Supra-Competencies', which break down into four categories of Intellectual, Interpersonal, Adaptability, and Results-Orientation. Between them, these twelve probably cover most of what comes up in all the other, often longer, lists of competencies.

## An evaluation of ACs

A lot of the faith in ACs is due to their high face validity — and also because of the scientific evidence in their favour, which is overwhelmingly positive in terms of their ability to predict career potential and success. However, neither of these means that an AC is actually doing a good job. It is just as easy to set up and run a bad AC as it is to carry out a poor interview. There are some appalling ACs being operated in the UK at the present time. So, one cannot generalise with ACs — because some are good, it does not mean they all are. If, however, they are set up and run in a careful and professional manner, and if they are subject to evaluation and monitoring, they are the best and most thorough method available.

The use of the ACs is quite flexible; they can be employed for assessing the potential of:

- junior and middle managers for more senior levels
- first line supervisors for junior/middle management
- scientific, professional and technical staff for general management or for management within their own specialism.

What they are not usually acceptable for is the more senior levels. Whilst there are exceptions (e.g. the board of one of the operating businesses of the Post Office), most senior managers are reluctant to engage in AC-type assessment procedures. The politics and status of operating at this level does create difficulties in running and assessing such things as group exercises. Senior managers are therefore more likely to be put through an external, psychometrically based, individual assessment procedure.

Some of the issues associated with ACs that were outlined above have led to an increasing use of a rather different version of the method, known as the Development Centre (DC). Essentially, this is similar in format to the AC, but the focus is much more on the training and development needs of the individual than on coming out with an overall rating of potential – indeed, no OAR is provided at all. The idea is to capitalise on the learning potential of the AC exercises and to use the information they generate to build a development plan for each participant. This largely removes the problem of some people being branded as failures or, come to that, as crown princes. The assessors may include more personnel, management development and training staff, though senior line managers will often still be involved. A further variation on this theme was developed some years ago in ICL, where they put together Self-Insight Assessment Centres (SIACs). The approach taken here was that the participants themselves helped in assessing one another, with the aim of increasing self-awareness and enhancing personal effectiveness. Other DCs have adopted this principle and include some elements of self-assessment. Though it is difficult to formally evaluate DCs in the way one can ACs, because their output is individually tailored and there is no clear-cut criterion against which to measure their success, experience suggests that they are extremely valuable to the participants.

## Assessing Potential: Summary and Conclusions

There is still a place for the annual appraisal in assessing promotability, but where the appraisal is of the traditional kind its role is a limited one. The way so many organisations have taken to using psychometric tests and assessment centres in recent years suggests that this point has been widely recognised. As a trend, it looks set to continue and strengthen for some time yet. One of the advantages of this kind of strategy is that it allows appraisal of performance to be very much line led, but puts the assessment of potential into a wider perspective that cannot usually be provided by line management alone. It also offers a superior level of objectivity and predictive power in assessment. If handled sensibly, tests and ACs can still leave line managers with a substantial role in implementing career development plans and decisions for their staff. Where it is felt that tests and ACs are not the most appropriate techniques, the development of behavioural inter- viewing has a lot to offer.

Whichever approach to assessing potential is used, it remains essential that there is an attempt to identify the needs of the organisation in the years ahead. The competencies or skill dimensions arrived at through such a process can be built into the appraisal of performance *and* potential, and a clearer picture will emerge of the likely career opportunities and pathways. With this information, both the organisation and its employees can take decisions and make plans. If the latter know what the options are, and have also been put through assessment methods that give them feedback about their skills and strengths, they are in a much stronger position to direct their own careers. Various techniques such as career planning workshops and workbooks can further help them in this respect; the reader is directed to Fletcher and Williams (1992, pages 50–63) or Mumford (1993) for a fuller discussion of these participative, self-directed methods.

# Chapter 9

# New frontiers for appraisal

One of the most marked trends in appraisal in recent years has been the extension of its coverage, touched on in Chapter 1. There have been two aspects to this: one was the way that existing company appraisal schemes were applied to cover more staff, including professional and technical groups (Long, 1986), and the other has been the wider adoption of performance appraisal in the public sector. Taking the first of these, the attitudes and characteristics of professional and scientific staff, whether in public or private sector organisations, are often so different from those of administrative and managerial staff that they represent a special case in appraisal. As far as the second aspect is concerned, 'adoption' may not be the most appropriate word, as in many instances appraisal has been introduced into the public sector as a result of government insistence and pressure. Ministers have seen it as a way of regulating and improving performance standards, and of raising service delivery levels. Some public sector organisations have had appraisal for a long period – the Civil Service first introduced a comprehensive scheme in the early 1970s – but for the most part it was a new concept to the National Health Service (NHS), the teaching profession, higher education and academia. Some local government bodies also developed more systematic appraisal schemes during this period. In all these cases, elements of PRP began to be introduced as well, again as a result of central government policy.

The main focus of this chapter will be on the appraisal of professional and scientific staff, but much of it will be in the context of the public sector. This is because there is a far higher proportion of professional staff in the NHS, the teaching profession, higher education and (to a lesser extent) local government than in the majority of commercial organisations. None the less, a fair amount of what is said about the appraisal of professional groups is applicable to their employment in the private

128

sector also. Before addressing the general and specific issues associated with the appraisal of such staff, it is relevant to make some points about public sector appraisal and where recent developments have led.

## Appraisal in the Public Sector

Accepting for the moment that talking in terms of the whole public sector is lumping together a wide range of fairly disparate organisations, is there any real reason for expecting appraisal to be different here than in the private sector? It could be argued that the vagaries of government policy and the way it affects the public sector are probably no greater than those of the market place and the City and their effects on the private sector. Large parts of the private sector are providing services, just as the public sector is. The types of organisational structures found in the two sectors have become more similar, too.

But there are some important distinctions to be drawn. To list just some of the main ones:

- Assessing the output and effectiveness of public sector organisations is much more complex than with the private sector. How society should judge the effectiveness of an individual police officer and of his police service as a whole is generally seen as a more contentious issue than how the effectiveness of managers and commercial companies are assessed.
- Much of the public sector has had to run appraisal on very limited resource budgets.
- More significantly, in many instances – teaching and higher education are notable examples – appraisal has been imposed directly as a result of government policy. This is certainly not a promising backdrop for setting up an appraisal scheme.
- In the health and educational fields (as we have already noted) there are large concentrations of professional staff organised in structures that have few hierarchical levels and where the concept of 'management' is somewhat alien.

The thrust of these differences is that it is often more challenging to make appraisal work well in the public sector.

Be that as it may, appraisal has been introduced. In the NHS, the appraisal is known by the term Individual Performance Review (IPR) and was first introduced in 1986. The IPR documentation is thorough and quite attractively produced. Evaluation of how the system has fared (Institute of Health Services Management, 1991) suggests that it has been moderately successful, though the emphasis on performance improvement seems to have been at the expense of improving personal development planning and job satisfaction. This imbalance raises some doubts about its long-term effectiveness. It is noteworthy that in private sector health care settings, rather different approaches to appraisal are taken; see, for example, Wilson and Cole's (1990) account of the way it operates in the Nuffield Hospitals group, which suggests a greater orientation towards self-assessment and development.

The recommendations and plans for school teacher appraisal have been published (HMSO, 1989; DES, 1991) and the scheme is operating. An evaluation study of pilot teacher-appraisal schemes helped guide the formulation of the policy adopted (Bradley *et al.*, 1989). The teachers' scheme has provision for both classroom observation of the teacher and the collection of peer reports on performance by the appraiser. In higher education, where appraisal was introduced a few years ago, there is more flexibility and variety in the way the schemes operate. There are, though, various recommendations to guide them (e.g. USDTU Report, 1990), and with the advent of the academic audit of quality, not to mention the increasing use of PRP, the role of appraisal is set to increase. Examination of the appraisal and performance management schemes run by local and central government organisations shows little in the way of consistent or substantial differences from those found in the private sector. As far as performance management schemes are concerned, there is some reason for believing that many public sector organisations − and particularly those in local government − are at least as advanced as those in the private sector (SOCPO, 1992).

This quick review serves to illustrate how far appraisal has already been implemented in these areas. It is, as noted earlier, even more challenging to make appraisal work well in the public sector. Despite that, the principles and practices outlined throughout this book are equally relevant in this context. The one major difference is perhaps in dealing with the professional and scientific staff groups that feature prominently in many public sector organisations, and it is to that topic we now turn.

## Appraisal Issues With Professional and Scientific Staff

The key to understanding some of the potential difficulties in making appraisal work with professional groups is to contrast the ethos of the professional with the ethos of organisations. The former is typified by:

- high levels of autonomy and independence of judgment
- self-discipline and adherence to professional standards
- the possession of specialised knowledge and skills
- power and status based on expertise
- operating, and being guided by, a code of ethics
- being answerable to the governing professional body.

There are other attributes, but these are the main ones. Where professionals operate within the context of a private practice or some other small professional grouping, there is no serious problem as all are working to the same model. Not so, however, where they work as part of a much larger and more general organisation. Listing the characteristics of the conventional organisational ethos immediately shows the conflict of value systems:

- hierarchical authority and direction from superiors
- administrative rules and procedures to be followed
- standards and goals defined by the organisation
- primary loyalty demanded by the organisation
- power based on legitimate organisational position.

Small wonder professionals experience role conflict at times, with different expectations and demands from their profession and from their organisational employers. For example, doctors and university lecturers are apt to see their work as being determined by the needs of their patients or students respectively, and by their professional training, rather than by the pragmatic considerations that drive so many organisational decisions on how resources are allocated. One university vice-chancellor summed up the problem very graphically and succinctly: he said that managing academics was like trying to shepherd a flock of cats! Much the same could be said of many professional groups; they do not take easily to the idea of being managed. There are of course variations in the extent to which this is true — for example, engineers are perhaps more used to working within commercial organisational management structures than are some other professions.

Appraisal is likely to fall right into the centre of this 'ethos gap'. It represents an organisational procedure that is embedded within a hierarchical authority structure; it frequently implies that some external agent or process is necessary to motivate and guide the individual's work; and it is the mechanism whereby the organisation's goals are imposed at lower levels. The kinds of performance measures that enter into appraisal discussions may well reflect outcomes that are of primary importance at organisational level but which seem misleading, crude or irrelevant to the professional. Thus, measures like the number of students enrolled, the number of patients seen or the number of social work cases covered are of limited importance to the professionals concerned without some meaningful check on how well quality has been maintained. The professional's aspiration is, more often than not, to achieve the highest standard possible and to extend professional skills and expertise in doing so. The organisation's goals, on the other hand, tend to be more about cost-effectiveness and delivering a reasonable product or service rather than the best possible, even in these quality-conscious days.

On top of all this, the appraisers may or may not be fellow professionals. Where they are not, there is a serious danger of a communication gap between the two parties; they start from different positions and speak different languages. Where professionals appraise one another, this problem does not usually exist, but instead, the organisational agenda for appraisal may well be ignored. Also, it is often the case that the whole process is perceived as embarrassing, as being inappropriate or even distasteful by both parties — with the consequence that it is not treated seriously and is carried out in a superficial manner.

The result of the differences between professional ethos and organisational ethos is to make appraisal far more difficult to introduce and run successfully. It is simply no use to try to operate the appraisal of professional and scientific staff as if they were no different from any others. Quite apart from the points already made, it has to be remembered that this is a group who have usually been through an extended qualification process, and they have a far higher level of educational achievement than most. This alone might serve to make them a more challenging prospect as far as appraisal is concerned. We can look at the detailed implications of all this for how appraisal functions with members of professional and scientific groups later in the chapter. But for the moment, a more general point has to be made. If performance appraisal in one form or another is to be part of the way these staff groups work and are managed, then it would be better to face head-on the issues of the conflicting value systems outlined above before any practical appraisal arrangements are put in place. If both the professionals concerned and the non-professional elements of the organisational management can discuss their expectations and differences at the outset – in seminars, consultative sessions, organisational development workshops or whatever – many of the problems can be addressed and perhaps minimised. They will not be eliminated, but raising awareness of the differing expectations can help in achieving some of the compromises necessary between organisational and individual goals if the appraisal process is to be constructive. The general requirement for performance appraisal to recognise the needs and values of appraisees and appraisers, rather than just the organisation's aims, is even stronger with professional groups.

## Designing and Implementing Appraisal for Professional Staff

### Designing appraisal

As can be gathered from the preceding paragraphs, getting the aims of appraisal right is both more difficult and even more crucial when professional groups are concerned. Potentially, appraisal can serve the same functions for this group as for other employees. However, two points need to be kept in mind:

- Professionals tend to be fairly high on self-motivation, and an overt emphasis on appraisal as a motivating device may cause it to be rejected as unnecessary.

- Assessment against professional and personal standards is acceptable, but is usually perceived as being more relevant to development than to deciding on rewards.

The organisation will generally want appraisal to be a means of directing the efforts of professional staff in such a way that they are in line with the main organisational objectives and priorities. This is far from straightforward: as we have seen, the kinds of performance criteria and outcomes that the organisation values are not always reflected in the views of the individual professional. What all this means is that the *presentation* of the aims of appraisal becomes almost as important as the aims themselves.

Appraisal is more likely to be acceptable if it is seen as a means of facilitating effective cooperation in achieving common goals and as a mechanism for improving professional development than if it is perceived as a way of assessing and motivating professionals to drive organisational performance. In the final analysis, there may not be much difference between these two perspectives in what they actually entail, but there may be a world of difference in how they are thought of. The language and terminology is thus of some significance here. The word 'appraisal' seems to have more negative connotations with professionals than it has for most people, probably because it is seen as something to do with industry and not relevant to their approach to work. Consequently, it may be wise to look for alternative terms. The most popular tend to be variations on a few themes:

- Individual Development Interviews
- Work Planning and Review Sessions
- Professional Development Interviews
- Performance Development Sessions
- Job Progress Reviews.

Any title that diminishes the implication that the session is about assessment is an improvement (of course, staff may still call it the appraisal anyway!).

So far, this discussion has treated all professional groups as being much the same. Whilst their similarities might outweigh their differences, the latter do exist. It cannot be assumed that where there is more than one professional group, they will all react in the same way. This was illustrated in Chapter 5 when it was recounted how local government engineers and social workers had been found to have rather different styles and preferences in relation to appraisal. These differences, too, have to be addressed in the design process, by ensuring that all the professional groups concerned are represented in the consultation exercise, and that they are made aware of the differing views of their colleagues in other professions. This is particularly beneficial, as professionals do sometimes need reminding that their own particular profession does not have a monopoly on wisdom. The main point here, though, is that it may make the consultation and design stage of appraisal slower where professional groups are involved than would normally be the case. That slower progress should be built in to the planned timetable for introducing appraisal. Trying to rush into implementation by short-cutting the discussion process is liable to leave a residue of problems.

It was noted earlier that the hierarchical authority structures of organisations do not always fit the professional's concept of control and discipline. This not only affects the aims of appraisal, but who should carry it out. The traditional notion of the immediate boss being the appraiser is called into question. If that boss is a member of the same profession as the appraisee, there is a considerable chance of them colluding to make it a non-event if they do not feel downward appraisal to be appropriate. Or it may focus exclusively on professional content — the appraisal may be seen as an opportunity to discuss arcane technical issues and to review career development and may therefore neglect the less intrinsically interesting matter of meeting objectives. If the boss is not a fellow professional, then the situation may be even worse — the appraiser can be viewed by the appraisee as lacking the knowledge and skills to make a valid judgment about performance, as well as not being in a position to offer career development advice. An additional problem is that, in some organisations dominated by professional staff, there are very few, and often ill-defined, layers of authority. The consequence is that where line management responsibility can be defined, the number of appraisees to each appraiser may be rather high. So, the question of who the appraiser should be therefore requires careful consideration. There are several options:

## 1. Allow choice

The idea of people choosing their appraisers is found in both teacher and (some) university appraisal schemes. As regards teachers, the practice is not encouraged, but is certainly allowable under some circumstances (DES, 1991). The virtue of letting people nominate their own appraisers is that they can pick those individuals who have most relevant knowledge of their work and their professional specialism, and whom they respect. There are certainly occasions where it can be appropriate to follow such a route: where there is no obvious immediate superior who is in a position to appraise; where the person works in a very highly specialised field; or where the numbers of staff to be appraised would be too great for the appraiser and some way has to be found to spread the load. Unfortunately, there are many potential problems that limit the value of taking this approach more generally. The main one is that appraisees may choose appraisers on less desirable grounds – personal friendship, or the knowledge that X is a 'soft touch' – which result in a less than thorough or constructive discussion. Even where they are chosen for more legitimate reasons, such appraisers may not be in a position to give the broader perspective and support necessary to help the appraisee. There are also administrative difficulties that arise if this choice process is allowed on a widespread basis. So, the principle of allowing choice of appraiser is useful in some special circumstances, but has to be carefully controlled – the choice needs to be sanctioned by whoever has responsibility for the appraisal process.

## 2. Multi-level, multi-source appraisal

Some general points on multiple appraisal were discussed in Chapter 5, and most of these also apply in appraising professionals. Again, this approach has been used in various forms in teaching and university appraisal (see Box 9.1 for the former).

---

**Box 9.1: Multiple appraisal for teachers**

Teachers' appraisal is based on a degree of self-assessment (encouraged but not compulsory), on at least two classroom

---

observation sessions, and on other sources of information including people who have knowledge of the individual's work. The latter vary according to the appraisee's position; they would be mainly peers for most teachers, but for head teachers could include governors, parents, and LEA officers. The appraiser has the task of approaching these sources, and is required by the regulations to consult the appraisee about it first. The DES circular (DES, 1991) says that 'during such consultation, appraisees should be given the opportunity to express their views about the principle of collecting information from the particular people involved and the method of collection'. The code of practice that is included in this document states that:

- Appraisers should act with sensitivity and not exhibit bias in collecting information.
- Appraisees should not adopt an obstructive attitude to reasonable proposals for collecting information.
- Neither appraisers nor appraisees should act in way that might undermine mutual trust and confidence.
- Those giving information to be used in an individual's appraisal should be prepared to acknowledge and substantiate the comments they make.
- Those making significantly critical comments 'should be asked to discuss them directly with the appraisee' before they are used in the appraisal.

This and other guidance given reflects some of the potential pitfalls of having the appraiser personally collect data from other sources of appraisal. Whether exhortations of the kind presented in the code of practice will be effective in achieving a constructive form of multiple appraisal remains to be seen; the principles espoused seem fair enough.

One other feature of the teachers' appraisal scheme is novel, and that is the classroom observation element. It is not normal practice in other spheres to make a point of specifically observing the appraisee's performance during set periods. It has the positive benefit of introducing a clear, job-relevant behavioural sample into the appraisal process. What is likely to be obtained from this is more a measure of maximal performance than of typical performance – the appraisees will presumably ensure that they are doing their best when the pre-arranged observation periods take place, though they will possibly feel under some pressure from being appraised so overtly. None the less, there is some value in being able to see what the individual is capable of, and it is an approach that could be adopted more widely. Whether repeating the exercise frequently is likely to add a great deal is perhaps more questionable.

The attraction of multiple appraisal to professional staff rests mainly on self- and peer-review, both of which fit the professional ethos much better than appraisal by superiors. In universities and in the scientific community, the peer review process has long been established and accepted as the best way of judging the merit of individual pieces of work and of assessing the suitability of people for promotion. However, it has to be noted that, in this context, the word 'peers' is often used to refer to members of the same professional group and specialism rather than necessarily to imply people of the same rank or level. Input to appraisal from colleagues working in the same professional field is acceptable because they are knowledgeable about that field and the individual's contribution to it, and not because they are in some sense senior or in a position of authority – their authority comes from expert power, not rank.

But the concept of multiple appraisal has wider implications for some professionals than it generally does for managers. It can include input from patients about the way they are dealt with by health care professionals, from students on the way they are taught by lecturers, and so on (there are limits to this – criminals' views on their arresting officers may be a touch biased). Where such sources of information are mooted, they are sometimes questioned on their capacity to offer objective or useful evidence. However, to take the case of lecturers as an example, the evidence shows that student ratings of their teachers are sufficiently reliable and valid (for example, they correlate quite highly with ratings of teaching ability made by superiors, peers and classroom observers) to use in feedback aimed at performance improvement and in personnel decision-making (Rushton and Murray, 1985). The problem with appraisal input from consumers of professional services is that getting it is usually time-consuming and sometimes costly. But with the growing focus on quality considerations, this is something that may well play a larger part in appraisal in the future, and not just with professionals.

## 3. Split-role appraisal

Sometimes an alternative is to have a form of multiple appraisal but in separate sessions – which might be called split-role appraisal. This is useful in addressing the problem of the appraisee having dual responsibilities and roles. On the one hand there is the professional specialism and all that it entails, and on the other there is the administrative and managerial role the individual may fill in the organisation. It is quite possible to have different appraisers for each, a professional mentor for the professional role and a senior manager for the organisational role. There are some difficulties with this, mainly in connection with the areas of interface and overlap, and it is more costly in resource terms, but it can work well enough, provided that the appraisers consult where necessary before and after the session.

### Appraisal training

The concept of training can receive a very mixed reception amongst professionals. Some see no difference in kind between attending an appraisal training course and the prolonged training they have already received for their professional career. Others see it as somewhat threatening. I well remember a college principal saying, when asked about the training to be given to appraisers in the institution: 'I do not like to use the word training. I prefer to think that we can deal with this through discussion meetings.' For some senior professionals, the idea of attending a skills-based appraisal course, with the attendant risk of being seen not to perform well (or, as they might think of it, of making a fool of themselves) in front of others may not be very appealing. In view of these mixed reactions, the first step in setting up appraisal training for professionals is to gauge their attitude to the idea, and to assess how much help − and in what form − the professionals concerned feel they need.

The briefing sessions that introduce the appraisal system can be used as a vehicle for assessing the demand for training. Such sessions may also have the function of examining some of the professional−organisational ethos differences, if these have not been brought out in a prior consultation process. Whilst it might be rather late in the day to bring these up, it is better that they are made explicit and thought about rather than simply ignored. The briefing sessions can be extended to have a more direct training function by going over guidance notes on how to handle the interview, discussing ways of dealing with problem performers and so on. This in itself can be used to raise awareness of the need for training, and to demonstrate its potential value. There is little point in forcing people to undergo training that they do not want, so being able to offer training to those that would like it, without it being mandatory (at least, initially), is a reasonable approach. For the others, after doing appraisals for the first time their attitudes can change and any resistance to the idea of skills training may decrease or disappear.

The actual form of appraisal training, where professional staff are involved, does not usually need to be any different from normal. However, there are some points to be aware of, and these are relevant to the briefing sessions, too. HR staff who have been involved in appraisal training in organisations with large numbers of scientific staff will tell you that the latter tend to apply their normal perspective on the world to appraisal as well: they will want some evidence that what is being presented to them works. This evidence can take the form of examples of how the same approach is used successfully elsewhere, in similar organisations of sufficient status for them to respect, and/or it can be in the form of academic research demonstrating that the principles embedded in the appraisal scheme are effective in achieving the desired ends. Any figures or statistics delivered in the course of this will be subject to careful scrutiny and evaluation. Concepts and assumptions will be examined in detail. All of which can make the delivery of appraisal training to groups of this kind fairly demanding for the trainers. They will need to be prepared to deal with questions of a rather different kind from scientific and professional staff, who are more inclined to focus on underlying principles than is the average manager.

There is also a need for trainers to be sensitive to likely differences between professional groups in how they react to appraisal. Typically, the more technically based professionals are prone to emphasising content and procedural issues. They often feel quite happy and comfortable with rating scales and quantitative measures, with appraisal that revolves around clear procedures and the completion of report forms. In contrast, experience suggests that the 'soft' professions and disciplines, those that deal with human and social issues in the main, are much more likely to react negatively to the quantitative aspects of appraisal and assessment. Instead, they direct their attention to the process aspects of appraisal, and show more concern about handling the interaction with the appraisee in a sensitive and conflict-free manner. Both groups and perspectives have their strengths and weaknesses. It is the task of the trainer to organise the appraisal training to cater for these. Two basic approaches are possible. One is to make sure that on any course, the participants are from a mixed group; the idea here is that they act as corrective influences on each other. The alternative is try to make the course membership group-specific and to gently shape the training in such a way as to counterbalance the biases of that particular group.

## Appraising Potential Amongst Professional Staff

There are, broadly speaking, two different pathways open to professionals: one is to make progress in their own specialism and reach positions of responsibility within the profession, while the other is to branch out into more generalist roles, where their training may still play a part in their work, albeit a steadily diminishing one. In the early career stage, the promotability of an individual will often be based on both professional competence and development, and on effectiveness in their organisational role. It is usually important for both these to be assessed and taken account of in the promotion decision. Sometimes they go hand-in-hand, and there is no great problem. It is not always the case, though, and many organisations – for example, those operating in the advanced technology field – find that some of their staff are so good technically that they have to be given career advancement on this basis alone (if the company is to keep them), even if their more general personal skills are seriously deficient. For other individuals, the balance tilts in the opposite direction. If this is the situation, then the appraisal process has some role in identifying both to the individual and to the organisation what the future career pattern is likely to be, so that everyone concerned knows where they stand. It seems essential here that the appraisal does include inputs from both professional and organisational perspectives.

As with other staff groups, appraisal does not itself offer a very satisfactory mechanism for making decisions on longer-term promotion potential. The alternative methods, reviewed in Chapter 8, can all be applied with professional groups. Of these, though, the assessment (or development) centre is perhaps the most appropriate. Its flexibility makes it possible to devise AC exercises that are designed to assess potential for managing professionals or exercises that are designed to assess potential for generalist management. The latter can be quite useful in acting as a realistic job preview, giving candidates a taste of what such work might be like and allowing them to decide whether they would want to go down this route.

# Chapter 10

## Appraisal: neither deadly disease nor panacea

Today, many organisations are structured very differently to how they would have been ten years ago. The implication of this is that performance appraisal *cannot* be the same as it was then and still claim to be relevant. The traditional model of a centrally devised and run appraisal system, with an emphasis on assessment and overall ratings of performance, applied to all staff in the same manner, is no longer appropriate to a high proportion of advanced companies, and is likely to be decreasingly suitable for many more in the next few years. The fact that it is no longer clear in many organisations as to who is the most appropriate person to be the appraiser for an individual is enough in itself to indicate how things have changed.

Perhaps it is not surprising if, with all these pressures and shifts in thinking that have taken place, some people question whether there is any place at all for appraisal in the modern organisation. No one has put this more strongly than the 'guru' of total quality, W. Edward Deming, who has identified performance appraisal as one of the seven deadly diseases of current management practice (Deming, 1986). The crux of his argument is that appraisal does harm because it leads to the erroneous perception that variations in performance are caused by individual employees, whereas the real situation is that such variations are caused by the systems created and controlled by managers. This leads to a focus on the wrong responses to quality shortcomings and to low morale amongst those appraised. Deming believes (a) that individuals do not differ significantly in terms of their performance, with such variation as there is being attributable to random observations and sampling error, (b) variations in performance are due mainly to factors outside the individual's control, and (c) managers cannot effectively differentiate between individuals and systems as the cause in performance variation. Deming's ideas have had widespread impact, and not just in relation to quality issues. Carson, Cardy and Dobbins (1991) report that in the USA, Ford have been experimenting with reducing the appraisal categories from nine to three; they have taken on Deming's point that most people perform within the limitations of the system, and have decided that only 5–11 per cent of staff should be rated higher or lower than the middle category.

Is Deming right? In most respects, he surely is. The inability of appraisers to assess accurately has been a consistent theme in this book, and much of what Deming says reflects the kind of attributional error described in Chapter 6 (page 76). The importance of other, external factors influencing individual performance was noted then, as it was when objective-setting was discussed in Chapter 3. Perhaps the only point of disagreement is his suggestion that there are no substantial differences between individuals in their performance. This flies in the face of a great deal of research on human performance across a wide range of settings. However, this contention on his part possibly does not matter much anyway from an appraisal viewpoint; if appraisers are not good at assessing performance differences and attributing them correctly, and if external factors are more important in determining performance than are individual capabilities, then there is little point in having performance appraisal based primarily on assessment.

Most of what Deming says, then, is in line with the argument presented throughout this book – that the traditional, assessment-oriented approach to appraisal, with its emphasis on comparing people and links with pay, fails to deliver on almost every count. It might well be regarded as a deadly disease, but it does *not* mean that other approaches to appraisal are equally lethal. This is where the name gets in the way. Calling these other approaches 'appraisal' does rather confuse the issue, but the generic title of appraisal still seems to be used (as it is in the title of this book) to cover them all. The only way for practice in this field to make any sense is to break appraisal down into two parts:

1. A *performance planning session* that involves reviewing achievement of objectives over the period in question and setting objectives for the period ahead. If PRP has to come into the picture – and this writer believes that, in the case of merit

pay, it would be better if it did not – this is what it is related to.

2. A *development review*, probably based on competencies or skill dimensions, that looks at the training and development needs of the individual, and which can feed into the assessment of potential (where the latter is done by other, more effective, methods). If a competency approach has been used, then those competencies can be reflected in selection, appraisal, training and in assessing potential (in ACs etc.).

This view of how appraisal should operate is not new; in various and sometimes rather different forms, it has been around since Meyer and his colleagues (Meyer, Kay and French, 1965) called for split roles in performance appraisal as a result of their work in the American company GEC in the 1960s. But it is far more relevant now than at any previous time. Organisations are increasingly knowledge based, and are focusing to a greater extent on training managers in learning techniques to help them become more flexible and adaptable – see Beard (1993) for an account of work of this kind in British Telecom. This, along with the flatter and more flexible management structures, and the need for greater self-reliance and autonomy in career planning, is beginning to produce the kind of situation and employee attitudes that have hitherto only been found in organisations characterised by a high proportion of professional staff amongst their workforce. In other words, some of the conflicts of ethos that were described in Chapter 9 in relation to professional staff in the public sector are likely to become more relevant in the private sector, too. Trying to persist with traditional appraisal approaches in these circumstances seems doomed to failure.

Performance appraisal centred on performance improvement and development, along the lines of the two-part process described above, is likely to be more successful. There is, of course, still a need to assess within the framework of such an approach, but it is not assessment done for its own sake, or as a primary purpose; it is simply a means to an end. The question of linking pay with performance remains a difficult one. In the approach being advocated here, it can be related to achievement against objectives, as already indicated, though perhaps the more promising way forward is for pay to be tied to *team* performance rather than to individual performance.

Although some of these ideas about splitting the functions of appraisal have been around for a while, the traditional, stand-alone, monolithic appraisal system is still with us, especially — and perhaps not surprisingly — in traditional British manufacturing companies. How can these and other companies be persuaded that they are wasting their time and resources in following an approach that has repeatedly been shown to be bankrupt? It is usually down to the HR department, and/or external consultants, to bring the message home. There are a number of strategies that can be used, individually or in concert, to effect change in this area:

- The use of questionnaire surveys of attitudes to management, to communications, to reward systems and to the current appraisal arrangements is often a powerful way of highlighting problems and the need to take action.
- The use of external examples is something that tends to hold senior management attention. Knowing what other, high-performing and respected companies are doing can have a salutary effect. No board of directors likes to feel that the company is looking dated and backward in its approach, and that (in particular) the competition is stealing a march on them. The HR department can be judicious in picking its examples for comparison!
- Using research findings on appraisal from studies done elsewhere can be quite useful in presenting a case in the more science and technology based companies. This can be done through written briefings, but is usually more effective if embedded within a presentation by ...
- Consultants and outside experts. Such people can make boardroom presentations about what is going on in appraisal and what the latest thinking is. They will often, and probably quite unjustifiably, be more listened to than would the organisation's own HR staff.
- Running a pilot study of a new appraisal scheme in one department can be an effective way of demonstrating the value of the approach and the principles it embodies. Having been shown it can work within the organisation is reassuring and persuasive to senior management.
- Getting senior management to participate in any kind of strategic analysis of where the organisation is going, what it will

look like in a few years' time, what sort of staff it will need, and so on, should inevitably lead to a re-consideration of how people are selected, appraised and developed. This kind of exercise may be facilitated by the HR department, with or without external consultants, and can be presented as part of organisational development as a whole (which it is) rather than as simply a mechanism for reviewing appraisal.

* The adoption of performance management within the organisation can act as a vehicle for the review of appraisal arrangements – indeed, it has to, as appraisal in one form or another is the pivotal mechanism of performance management.

The HR professionals are almost always the key facilitators in bringing about changes in appraisal. Making appraisal a line-led activity actually strengthens their hand. They are in the position to guide and support, rather than being in the invidious role of demanding and enforcing. They will have access to much wider knowledge and expertise in the area than will the line managers, and they can use this to great effect in shaping what is set up and how it runs. By involving the line in setting the agenda for appraisal and in determining how it will run, the HR department is able to work alongside them in a more cooperative and positive relationship than is the case where appraisal is seen as an activity imposed by personnel and for personnel.

## In Conclusion

Performance appraisal does not have to be a deadly disease, but nor is it likely to be a panacea. The dangers of expecting too much from it are still real. It can contribute more effectively when integrated into the framework of a performance management system, and in these circumstances looks likely to achieve more from the organisation's point of view than it ever would by itself. Yet despite becoming a little more sophisticated, performance appraisal remains fairly crude. Part of the problem is that the level of understanding of what motivates people at work is not all that it might be. I greatly enjoyed the contribution from the floor at the end of a paper given at the IPM National Conference; the speaker rose and said, with complete confidence, that there are only two things that motivate people – fear and greed. The thinking behind some appraisal systems is obviously based on a similar premise. However, until we can do somewhat better than at present in our analysis, it is going to remain difficult to make appraisal fully effective as a motivating force. Giving greater emphasis to understanding motivation in appraisal training will help, but more research is also needed to improve our basic knowledge.

Taking the wider picture, there are other issues that need to be addressed about what can realistically be expected from appraisal. The lessening of central control in organisations and the empowerment of employees places more responsibility than ever on the shoulders of the individual. There is a danger here that the pressures can get out of proportion, and it is no coincidence that all the social and organisational changes referred to in this book have been accompanied by a burgeoning concern – backed up by evidence – about the levels of work stress. Better performance does not come from simply setting goals, giving a small amount of extra financial reward and exhorting people to go for improved quality and customer care. It comes from a better and more even relationship, or contract, between organisations and individuals, one that recognises individual differences in needs and capacities, and which accepts that, beyond certain levels, asking more of people is actually counter-productive. So, alongside the performance culture and the learning organisation, we have to put something else – the caring organisation. Only within that kind of environment will appraisal realise its full potential for offering routes to improved performance.

# References

ANSTEY E., FLETCHER, C., and WALKER, J. (1976) *Staff Appraisal and Development*. Allen & Unwin: London.

BEARD, D. (1993) 'Learning to Change Organisations'. *Personnel Management*, January, pp. 32–35.

BEVAN, S. and THOMPSON, M. (1991) 'Performance Management at the Crossroads'. *Personnel Management*, November, pp. 36–39.

BOYATZIS, R. (1982) *The Competent Manager*. Wiley: New York.

BRADLEY, H., BOLLINGTON, R., DADDS, M., HOPKINS, D., HOWARD, J., SOUTHWORTH, G., and WEST, M. (1989) *Report on the Evaluation of the School Teacher Appraisal Pilot Study*. Cambridge Institute of Education.

CARSON, K. P., CARDY, R. L. and DOBBINS, G. H. (1991) 'Performance Appraisal as Effective Management or as Deadly Management Disease: Two Initial Empirical Investigations. *Group and Organization Studies*, 16, pp. 143–159.

CIVIL SERVICE DEPARTMENT (1978) *Application of Race Relations Policy in the Civil Service*. HMSO: London.

COCKERILL, T. (1989) 'The Kind of Competence for Rapid Change'. *Personnel Management*, September, pp. 52–56.

COOK, J. D. and WALL, T. D. (1980) 'New Work Attitude Measures of Trust, Organisational Commitment, and Personal Need Non-fulfilment'. *Journal of Occupational Psychology*, 53, pp. 39–52.

COOK, J. D., HEPWORTH, S. J., WALL, T. D. and WARR, P. B. (1981) *The Experience of Work*. Academic Press: London.

DEMING, W. E. (1986) *Out of the Crisis*. MIT Institute for Advanced Engineering Study: Cambridge, Mass.

DEPARTMENT OF EDUCATION AND SCIENCE (1991) *School Teacher Appraisal*. Circular 12/91, 12 July. DES: London.

DULEWICZ, S. V., FLETCHER, C., and WALKER, J. (1976) 'Job Appraisal Reviews Three Years On'. *Management Services in Government*, 31, pp. 1–11.

DULEWICZ, S. V. and FLETCHER, C. (1989) 'The Context and Dynamics of Performance Appraisal'. In HERRIOT, P. (*ed.*) *Assessment and Selection in Organisations*. John Wiley & Son: London

DULEWICZ, S. V. (1989) 'Assessment Centres as the Route to Competence'. *Personnel Management*, November, pp. 56–59.

DULEWICZ, S. V. and HERBERT, P. (1992) 'Personality, Competences Leadership Style and Managerial Effectiveness'. *Henley Management College Working Paper Series*, HWP 14/92.

DUNNETTE, M. D., CAMPBELL, J. P. and HELLERVIK, L. W. (1968) *Job Behaviour Scales for Penney Co. Department Managers*. Personnel Decisions: Minneapolis.

EDER, R. W. and FERRIS, G. R. (1989) *The Employment Interview*. Sage: Beverly Hills.

EGAN, G. (1990) *The Skilled Helper: A Systematic Approach to Effective Helping*. 4th ed. Brooks Cole.

FALCONER, H. (1991) 'Periodical Review'. *Personnel Today*, 23 July, p. 19.

FLANAGAN, J. C. (1954) 'The Critical Incident Technique'. *Psychological Bulletin*, 51, pp.327–58.

FLETCHER, C. (1978) 'Manager–subordinate Communication and Leadership Style: A field study of their relationship to perceived outcomes of appraisal interviews'. *Personnel Review*, 7, pp. 59–62.

FLETCHER, C. and DULEWICZ, S. V. (1984) 'An Empirical Study of a UK-based Assessment Centre'. *Journal of Management Studies*, 21, pp. 83–97.

FLETCHER, C. (1989) 'Impression Management in the Selection Interview'. In GIACALONE, R. A and ROSENFELD, P. (*eds*) *Impression Management in the Organisation*. Erlbaum: Hillsdale, NJ.

FLETCHER, C. (1991) 'Candidates' Reactions to Assessment Centres and Their Outcomes: A longitudinal study'. *Journal of Occupational Psychology*, 64, pp. 117–127.

FLETCHER, C. (1992) 'Quality Indicators in the Use of Psychometric Tests'. *Selection and Development Review*, 8, pp. 1–3.

FLETCHER, C. and WILLIAMS, R. (1992) *Performance Appraisal and Career Development*. 2nd ed. Stanley Thornes: Cheltenham.

FLETCHER, C. and KERSLAKE, C. (1993) 'Candidate Anxiety Level and Assessment Centre Performance'. *Journal of Managerial Psychology*, 8, In Press.

GAPPER, J. (1991) 'W H Smith to Retrain Managers in Motivation'. *Financial Times*, 8 May, p. 12.

GARLAND, H. and PRICE, K. H. (1977) 'Attitudes towards Women in Management, and Attributions of Their Success and Failure in Managerial Positions'. *Journal of Applied Psychology*, 62, pp. 29–33.

GAUGLER, B. B. ROSENTHAL D. B., THORNTON G. C. and BENTSON C. (1987) 'Meta-analysis of assessment centre validity'. *Journal of Applied Psychology Monograph*, 72, pp.493–511.

GEORGE, J. (1986) 'Appraisal in the Public Sector: Dispensing with the big stick'. *Personnel Management*, May, pp. 32–35.

GLAZE, T. (1989) 'Cadbury's Dictionary of Competence'. *Personnel Management*, July, pp. 44–48.

GREATREX, J. and PHILLIPS, P. (1989) 'Oiling the Wheels of Competence'. *Personnel Management*, August, pp. 36–39.

HARRIS, M. M. (1989) 'Reconsidering the Employment Interview: A review of recent literature and suggestions for future research'. *Personnel Psychology*, 42, pp. 691–726.

HILTON, P. (1992) 'Using Incentives to Reward and Motivate Employees'. *Personnel Management*, September, pp. 49–52.

HMSO (1978) *Applications of Race Relations Policy in the Civil Service*. Civil Service Department.

HMSO (1989) *School Teacher Appraisal: A National Framework*. HMSO: London.

HOFSTEDE, G. (1980) 'Motivation, leadership and organisation; do American theories apply abroad?' *Organizational Dynamics*, Summer.

HOLDSWORTH, R. (1991) 'Appraisal'. In NEALE, F. (*ed.*) *The Handbook of Performance Management*. Institute of Personnel Management: London.

INSTITUTE OF HEALTH SERVICES MANAGEMENT (1991) *Individual Performance Review in the NHS*. IHSM: London.

INSTITUTE OF PERSONNEL MANAGEMENT (1992) *Performance Management in the UK: An Analysis of the Issues*. IPM: London.

JACKSON, D. and ROTHSTEIN, M. (1993) 'Evaluating Personality Testing in Personnel Selection'. *The Psychologist*, 6, pp. 8–11.

JACOBS, R. (1989) 'Getting the Measure of Managerial Competence'. *Personnel Management*, October, pp. 32–37.

JONES, R. (1990) 'Integrating Selection in a Merged Company'. *Personnel Management*, September, pp. 38–42.

KANE, J. S. and LAWLER, E. E. (1978) 'Methods of Peer Assessment'. *Psychological Bulletin*, 85, pp. 555–586.

LATHAM, G. P. and SAARI, L. M. (1984) 'Do people do what they say? Further studies on the situational interview'. *Journal of Applied Psychology* 69, pp. 569–73.

LATHAM, G. P., SAARI, L. M., PURSELL, E. D. and CAMPION, M. A. (1980) 'The Situational Interview'. *Journal of Applied Psychology*, 65, pp. 422–427.

LATHAM, G. P. and LEE, T. W. (1986) 'Goal Setting'. In LOCKE, E. (*ed.*) *Generalising from Laboratory to Field Settings*. Lexington Books.

LATHAM, G. P. (1989) 'The Reliability, Validity, and Practicality of the Situational Interview'. In EDER, R. W. and FERRIS, G. R. (*eds*) *The Employment Interview*. Sage: Beverly Hills.

LOCKE, E. A., SHAW, K. N., SAARI, L. M. and LATHAM, G. P. (1981) 'Goal Setting and Task Performance: 1969–1980'. *Psychological Bulletin*, 90, pp. 125–152.

LOCKE, E. A. and HENNE, D. (1986) 'Work Motivation Theories'. In COOPER, C. and ROBERTSON, I. (*eds*) *International Review of Industrial and Organizational Psychology 1986*. Wiley: Chichester.

LODAHL, T. M. and KEJNER, M. (1965) 'The Definition and Measurement of Job Involvement'. *Journal of Applied Psychology*, 49, pp. 24–33.

LONG, P. (1986) *Performance Appraisal Revisited*. Institute of Personnel Management: London.

MABE, P. A. and WEST, S. G. (1982). 'Validity of self-evaluation of ability: A review and meta-analysis'. *Journal of Applied Psychology*, 67, 280–296.

MABEY, W. (1992) 'The Growth of Test Use'. *Selection and Development Review*, 8, Pt3, pp. 6–8.

MACDONNEL, R. (1989) 'Management by Objectives'. In HERRIOT, P. (ed.) *Assessment and Selection in Organizations*. Wiley: Chichester.

MCBEATH, G. (1990) *Practical Management Development*. Blackwell: Oxford.

152     *Appraisal*

McEVOY, G. M. (1988) 'Evaluating the Boss'. *Personnel Administrator*, 33, pp. 115–119.

McEVOY, G. M. (1990) 'Public Sector Managers' Reactions to Appraisal by Subordinates'. *Public Personnel Management*, 19, pp. 201–212.

MEYER, H. H., KAY, E. and FRENCH, J. R. P. (1965) 'Split Roles in Performance Appraisal'. *Harvard Business Review*, 43, pp. 123–129.

MEYER, H. H. (1980) 'Self-appraisal of Job Performance'. *Personnel Psychology*, 33, pp. 291–295.

MOWDAY, R. T., STEERS, R. M. and PORTER, L. W. (1979) 'The Measurement of Organisational Commitment'. *Journal of Vocational Behaviour*, 14, pp. 224–247.

MUMFORD, A. (1993) *Management Development: Strategies for Action.* Institute of Personnel Management: London.

NAPIER, N. K. and LATHAM, G. P. (1986) 'Outcome Expectancies of People Who Conduct Performance Appraisals'. *Personnel Psychology*, 39, pp. 827–837.

NATHAN, B. R., MOHRMAN, A. M. and MILLIMAN, J. (1991) 'Interpersonal Relations as a Context for the Effects of Appraisal Interviews on Performance and Satisfaction: A longitudinal study'. *Academy of Management Journal*, 34, pp. 352–369.

NEALY, S. M. (1964) 'Determining Worker Preferences among Employee Benefit Programs'. *Journal of Applied Psychology*, 48, pp. 7–12.

PEARCE, J. L. and PORTER, L. W. (1986) 'Employee Responses to Formal Appraisal Feedback'. *Journal of Applied Psychology*, 71, pp. 211–218.

PEARN, M. and KANDOLA, R. (1988) *Job Analysis: A Practical Guide for Managers.* Institute of Personnel Management: London.

RANDELL, G. A. (1980) 'The Skills of Staff Development'. In SPURGEON, W. T. and STAMMERS, R. B. (*eds*) *The Analysis of Social Skill.* Plenum: New York.

RANDELL, G. A., PACKARD, P. M. A. and SLATER, A. J. (1984) *Staff Appraisal: A First Step to Effectiveness.* 3rd ed. Institute of Personnel Management: London.

REDMAN, T. and SNAPE, E. (1992) 'Upward and Onward: Can staff appraise their managers?' *Personnel Review*, 21, pp. 32–46.

ROBERTSON, I. T. and MAKIN, P. J. (1986) 'Management Selection in Britain: A survey and critique'. *Journal of Occupational Psychology*, 59, pp. 45–58.

ROBERTSON, I. T., SMITH, M. and COOPER, C. L. (1992) *Motivation: Strategies, Theory & Practice.* 2nd ed. Institute of Personnel Management: London.

RODGERS, R. and HUNTER, J. E. (1991) 'Impact of Management by Objectives on Organisational Productivity'. *Journal of Applied Psychology Monograph*, 76, pp. 322–335.

RUSHTON, J. P. and MURRAY, H. G. (1985). 'On the Assessment of Teaching Effectiveness in British Universities'. *Bulletin of the British Psychological Society*, 38, pp. 361–365.

SCOTT, B. (1983) 'Evolution of an Appraisal Programme'. *Personnel Management*. August, pp. 28–30.

SHACKLETON, V. J. and NEWALL, S. (1991) 'Management Selection: A comparative survey of methods used in top British and French companies'. *Journal of Occupational Psychology*, 64, pp. 23–36.

SHEARD, A. (1992) 'Learning to Improve Performance'. *Personnel Management*, November, pp. 40–45.

SHRAUGER, J. S., and OSBERG, T. M. (1981) 'The relative accuracy of self-predictions and judgments by others in psychological assessment'. *Psychological Bulletin*, 90, pp. 322–351.

SLIVINSKI, L. W. and BOURGEOIS, R. P. (1977) 'Feedback of Assessment Centre Results'. In MOSES, J. L. and BYHAM, W. C. (eds) *Applying the Assessment Centre Method*. Pergamon: New York.

SMITH, P. C. and KENDALL, L. M. (1963) 'Retranslation of Expectations'. *Journal of Applied Psychology*, 47, pp. 149–155.

SOCIETY OF CHIEF PERSONNEL OFFICERS [SOCPO] (1992) *Performance Management Systems in Local Government*. Institute of Personnel Management: London.

SOFER, C. and TUCHMAN, M. (1970) 'Appraisal Interviews and the Structure of Colleague Relations'. *Sociological Review*, 8, pp. 365–392.

STINSON, J. and STOKES, J. (1980) 'How to Multi-appraise'. *Management Today*, June, pp. 43–53.

SUMMERS, D. (1991) 'BP Exploration Staff to Assess Managers' Work.' *Financial Times*, 7 May, p. 10.

TOPLIS, J., DULEWICZ, S. V. and FLETCHER, C. (1991) *Psychological Testing: A Manager's Guide*. Institute of Personnel Management: London.

USDTU (1990) *Appraisal in Universities – A Progress Report on the Introduction of Appraisal into the Universities in the United Kingdom*. Committee of Vice Chancellors & Principals/Universities' Staff Development Unit: London.

VROOM, V. J. (1964) *Work and Motivation*. Wiley: New York.

WALKER, J. (1989) 'The Appraisal Interview'. In Herriot, P. (*ed*.) *Assessment and Selection in Organizations*. Wiley: Chichester.

WALTERS, M. (1990) *What About the Workers? Making employee surveys work*. Institute of Personnel Management: London.

WARR, P. B. and BIRD, M. W. (1968) *Identifying Supervisory Training Needs*. HMSO: London.

WARR, P. B., COOK, J. and WALL, T. D. (1979) 'Scales for the Measurement of Some Work Attitudes and Aspects of Psychological Well-being'. *Journal of Occupational Psychology*, 52, pp. 129–148.

WEISNER, W. H. and CRONSHAW, S. F. (1988) 'A mete-analytic investigation of the impact of interview format and degree of structure on the validity of the employment interview'. *Journal of Occupational Psychology*, 84, pp. 275–90.

WILLIAMS, R. (1981) *Career Management and Career Planning*. HMSO: London.

WILLIAMS, R. and WALKER, J. (1985) 'Sex Differences in Performance Ratings: A research note'. *Journal of Occupational Psychology*, 58, pp. 331–337.

WILLIAMS, R. (1989) 'Alternative Raters and Methods'. In HERRIOT, P. (*ed*.) *Assessment and Selection in Organizations*. Wiley: Chichester.

WILSON, J. and COLE, G. 'A healthy approach to performance appraisal'.

Personnel Management, June, pp. 46–49.

WOODRUFFE, C. (1990) *Assessment Centres: Identifying and developing Competence*. IPM: London.

WRIGHT, P. M., LICHTENFELS, P. A. and PURSELL, E. D. (1989) 'The Structured Interview: Additional studies and a meta-analysis'. *Journal of Occupational Psychology*, 62, pp. 191–199.

WRIGHT, V. (1991) 'Performance-related Pay'. In NEALE, F. (*ed.*) *The Handbook of Performance Management*. Institute of Personnel Management: London.

ZEDECK, S. and BAKER, H. T. (1972) 'Nursing Performance as Measured by Behavioural Expectation Scales: A multitrait-multirater analysis'. *Organisational Behaviour and Human Performance*, 7, pp. 457–466.

# Appendix A:

## Example of appraisal scheme documentation

The appraisal documentation presented here, and the scheme it describes, is not in any sense supposed to be a 'model' for others to follow. It simply provides an example of a fairly basic and straightforward approach to appraisal that incorporates a fair amount of involvement and self-appraisal on the part of the appraisee. It contains an element of objective-setting, but avoids the use of rating scales and does not seek to come up with some overall performance measure. The amount of paperwork is kept to a minimum. Variations of it have been used successfully in both private and public sectors in past years, but it does represent a rather minimal approach in the sense that it stands alone and is not closely linked with other HR procedures or with business planning as a whole.

This example also provides an illustration of some of the more detailed guidance that may be given to appraisers about how to handle the appraisal interview. Normally, one would hope that this simply summarises what would have been put over in proper appraisal training.

# ANYCO LTD.

## Performance Appraisal Scheme
## Appraisers' Notes for Guidance

### Aim of the Appraisal Scheme

The purpose of the company appraisal scheme is to make the most effective use of its staff resources by developing them in a systematic way, in the interests both of the company and of the individuals being appraised. It provides those appraised with a formal opportunity to present what they feel to be their main achievements over the last year, to discuss their performance in general and to make plans for the year ahead. The scheme is a highly participative one, with a great deal of emphasis on self-appraisal, ensuring that staff have a major role in determining their own development. It is also very much future-oriented, being chiefly concerned with setting objectives and with improving performance.

One of the most frequent problems that arises with appraisals is that they become too closely identified with pay and promotion. Inevitably, there is a link between appraisal and rewards, but it is by no means a direct one. In terms of merit pay, appraisal is but one input to the decision − several other factors are taken into account. In the case of promotion, this is based on performance over a number of years, not just one. It is therefore of prime importance that the appraisal session is conducted in such a way that it emphasises (a) the development of the individual in the more immediate future, rather than the longer-term issue of promotion (b) the establishment of priorities and achievement of aims that reflect not only the needs of the individual, but also the wider needs of the company.

What follows is a guide to the appraisal process, and should be looked at in conjunction with the appraisal forms.

## Procedure

- Hand the appraisee the Self-appraisal Form and agree a date for the actual appraisal discussion, preferably in about a week's time. Check that the individual concerned has got a copy of the Guidance Notes for Appraisees.
- The appraisal discussion takes place, centred on the headings of the Self-appraisal Form.
- On the basis of this discussion, the agreed main action points and objectives for the year ahead are subsequently noted on the Appraisal Review Form by the appraiser.
- Return the completed Appraisal Review Form to the appraisee for signature as a correct record of the action points, aims and priorities.
- Give a copy of the Appraisal Review Form to the appraisee, keep a copy for yourself, and send one to Personnel.

## Preparing the Appraisal Session

Your starting point will be the headings of the different sections of the Self-appraisal Form. Most of these are straightforward enough and need no further explanation here. There are some points that need to be kept in mind when reviewing it, however:

- In Section 1, the appraisees are being asked to list their main responsibilities as they see them. It is always worth starting an appraisal discussion by checking that you and the appraisee have the same picture of what the job actually entails at the present time; it is very easy for it to have changed (particularly in a period of rapid development) without one or both parties fully appreciating the fact. *What do you expect to see written here?*
- The objectives set in the previous appraisal need to be reviewed, and the appraisees have been asked to look back at these under the second section heading of the Self-appraisal Form. *In preparing, you need to assess the objectives in terms of the extent to which they have been met, exceeded or not achieved.* What evidence are your assessments based on?
- Sections 3 and 4 ask the appraisees to look back and identify the strengths they have demonstrated and the areas where they feel

they could improve. It is important here to recognise that the appraisees are being invited to assess themselves by their own standards, not to compare themselves with other people. In other words, an individual may feel that he/she could have done certain things better, but that does not necessarily mean they have done them any less well than anyone else would have. Correspondingly, because someone has identified what they feel to be a strength does not of itself mean they have performed better in that respect than have their peers. *You will wish to give some thought to what you see as the more and less positive aspects of the individual's performance in the period under review.*

- Under Section 6, the appraisees have been invited to think about their main objectives for the year ahead. Taking account of the Business Plan and the departmental objectives, *what do you feel should be the key objectives for each appraisee?*

## The Appraisal Interview

The appraisal interview will take the headings of the Self-appraisal Form as its starting point, so the person appraised has a major responsibility for making the discussion a fruitful and constructive one. However, the more effort both parties have put in to preparing the interview, the more they will get out of it. There is no one correct way to handle an appraisal interview, but there are some general guidelines that can be given; if followed, they will help you carry out an effective interview and to avoid some of the most common pitfalls.

- Clear an adequate period of time for the discussion (better to err on the side of too long than too short, so 2 hours would not be inappropriate). Make sure that you will not be interrupted during the interview.
- Start by reminding the appraisee of the purpose of the appraisal and of the interview; make clear that you consider this as an important review process.
- Use the Self-appraisal Form as an agenda, and work through its headings. You may find it best to take them in the sequence printed, but there is no need to stick to this rigidly. There is no

requirement for the appraisee to actually show you what he/she has written on the form.

- Throughout the interview, put the onus on the appraisee to make the running. Ask the individual to expand on his/her own comments under each section of the form as you deal with them. When the appraisee has had the opportunity to say his/her own piece, add your own comments and discuss the issues generally.
- Do the achievements and the areas where the person feels he/she has done less well coincide with your own perceptions of their performance? If there are any significant discrepancies, they will have to be discussed. *Make sure you are considering the whole period under review — and not just what has happened recently.*
- Be sure to give full recognition to the appraisee's achievements and strengths; note specific examples of good work. It is particularly helpful to express appreciation of tasks which have not come easily and which have called for real effort or persistence on the individual's part.
- When tackling performance weaknesses (remember that they may be aspects of the person's performance that are only weak in comparison with that individual's overall performance, and not weak in comparison with other people), commend appraisees for their frankness where they have identified real shortcomings. Discuss them firmly but constructively, as ever trying as far as possible to get the appraisees to produce their own ideas and plans for overcoming the problems. There may be cases where the weaknesses mentioned by the appraisee on the Self-appraisal Form do not reflect the deficiencies in performance that you have identified. In such instances, you will need to address the difference of views in the appraisal discussion. Where an individual has identified an aspect of performance that has fallen short of their own standards but which you perceive as being perfectly satisfactory, little more than some reassurance may be needed. Potentially the most difficult disagreement is where you perceive weakness that the appraisee does not. In dealing with a situation of this kind:
  - be specific; make sure you have evidence to back up your comments — do not make vague and unsupported assertions
  - try to be firm but positive, keeping the emphasis on what constructive action can be taken; the aim is to improve performance, not to demotivate the individual

- do not tackle more than two areas of weakness in any depth; this is as much as most people can take without becoming defensive
- confine your comments to remediable weaknesses; there is little point in commenting on aspects of the individual which are not amenable to change. The emphasis is on appraising job performance, not the appraisee's personality.

- In identifying what action could be taken to improve performance (Section 5 of the form), has the individual made suggestions that are realistic and practical? To what extent has he/she taken responsibility for the action needed as opposed to projecting it on to others?
- Section 6 asks for suggestions on the objectives for the year ahead. You will want to evaluate and (through discussion) possibly modify these suggested objectives in terms of:
  - how demanding they are
  - how they relate to the individual's personal development
  - how they relate to the wider picture of the department's and the company's objectives and priorities, and any anticipated developments in the near future
  - how their achievement can be measured, where appropriate, in terms of both *time* and *end results*.
- Where there are some changes to the individual's responsibilities being suggested, be sure to put them in the wider context of the needs of both department and the company.
- When discussing training and development needs, look back at what has been identified as being the individual's relative strengths and weaknesses; how can the former be capitalised on, and how can the latter be improved through formal training, changes in duties, etc.? Amongst other things, you should also consider the likely work demands in the period ahead and reflect on whether these will call for updating existing skills or knowledge or the development of new capabilities on the appraisee's part. Be careful not to make promises on development issues that cannot be fulfilled.
- At the end of the interview, summarise the main points of the discussion; in particular, each party should summarise what action they have agreed to take and what should be entered on the Appraisal Review Form. Make sure that the appraisee has nothing further to raise.

- The Appraisal Review Form may be completed in the interview itself, or very shortly thereafter (in which case, return it to the individual quickly for signature, while the discussion is still fresh in mind). Both parties sign the form and keep copies.

## Self-appraisal Form Section Headings

1. Briefly list the main responsibilities of your job, and roughly what % of your time is spent on each.

2. Looking back to the objectives agreed at the last appraisal, which ones have been (a) exceeded, (b) met, (c) not achieved? What evidence have you to base these assessments on?

3. What do you feel you have done particularly well BY YOUR OWN STANDARDS over the last 12 months?

4. What do you feel you have done least well BY YOUR OWN STANDARDS over the past 12 months?

5. To help improve your performance in the job still further, what additional steps could be taken by:

   (a) you
   (b) your boss
   (c) others in the company.

6. What are your principal objectives for the year ahead? List four or five.

7. What changes, if any, in your responsibilities would you like to see in the near future?

8. What training and other steps could be taken to further your career development?

9. Is there anything else you wish to raise in the appraisal?

## Appraisal Review Form Headings

1. Review of past objectives:

   *Objectives*     *Extent Achieved*     *Measures/Evidence*

2. Action to be taken by:

   (a) The appraisee
   (b) The appraiser
   (c) Others in the company

3. Objectives for the coming year:

   *Objective*      *Priority*             *Form of Measurement*

   1.
   2.
   3.
   4.
   5.

Signed as an agreed record:

   *Appraisee*

   *Appraiser*

   *Date*

# ANYCO LTD.

## Performance Appraisal Scheme
## Appraisees' Notes for Guidance

### Aim of the Appraisal Scheme

The purpose of the company appraisal scheme is to make the most effective use of its staff resources by developing them in a systematic way, in the interests both of the company and of the individuals being appraised. It provides those appraised with a formal opportunity to present what they feel to be their main achievements over the last year, to discuss their performance in general and to make plans for the year ahead. The scheme is a highly participative one, with a great deal of emphasis on self-appraisal, ensuring that staff have a major role in determining their own development. It is also very much future-oriented, being chiefly concerned with setting objectives and with improving performance.

One of the most frequent problems that arises with appraisals is that they become too closely identified with pay and promotion. Inevitably, there is a link between appraisal and rewards, but it is by no means a direct one. In terms of merit pay, appraisal is but one input to the decision – several other factors are taken into account. In the case of promotion, this is based on performance over a number of years, not just one. It is therefore of prime importance that the appraisal session is conducted in such a way that it emphasises (a) the development of the individual in the more immediate future, rather than the longer-term issue of promotion, (b) the establishment of priorities and achievement of aims that reflect not only the needs of the individual, but also the wider needs of the company.

What follows is a guide to the appraisal process, and should be looked at in conjunction with the appraisal forms.

## Procedure

1. You and the appraiser agree a date for the appraisal discussion, preferably in about a week's time. The appraiser will give you a copy of the Self-appraisal Form.
2. You complete the Self-appraisal Form.
3. The appraisal discussion takes place, centred on the headings of the Self-appraisal Form. You do not need to give the form itself to the appraiser.
4. On the basis of this discussion, the agreed main action points and objectives for the year ahead are subsequently noted on the Appraisal Review Form by the appraiser, who returns it to you for signature as a correct record. Both of you keep copies.

## Completing the Self-appraisal Form

The headings are straight-forward enough, but there are some additional points that need to be made by way of guidance:

- In Section 1, you are being asked to list your main responsibilities as you see them, and to give a rough estimate of the % of time you spend on them. It is always worth starting an appraisal discussion by checking that you and the appraiser have the same picture of what the job actually entails at the present time; it is very easy for it to have changed (particularly in a period of rapid development) without one or both parties fully appreciating the fact.
- You need to look back at last year's appraisal form and confirm the objectives agreed. The extent to which these objectives have been achieved will be discussed, along with the circumstances that have had an impact on your performance, under the second section heading.
- Sections 4 and 5 ask you to identify what you have done best during the period under review and the areas where you feel you could have done better. It is important here to recognise that you are being invited to assess yourself by your own standards, not to compare yourself with other people. In other words, you may feel that you could have done certain things better (nobody is perfect!), but that does not necessarily mean you have done

them less well than anyone else would have. Try to pick out the two or three most important things under each heading.

- In completing Section 5, make your suggestions as realistic and practical as possible; resist the temptation to suggest the complete reorganisation of the company or changing government policy!

- When listing your main objectives for the period ahead under Section 6, consider how you would like to measure your success in achieving them; they will be reviewed again at the next appraisal, where appropriate (in some instances, circumstances may have changed in such a way as to make the objectives less relevant). The objectives set should reflect priorities for performance development rather than simply routine work. In framing them, consider the wider perspective of the needs of your department and of the company as a whole.

- The question of what changes you would like to see in your responsibilities in the future must, again, be tempered by realism (Section 7). The appraiser may of course have some suggestions to make in this context.

- Section 8 deals with training and development. In thinking about your needs in this area, look back at what you identified as being the strengths you identified in Section 3 – how can these be capitalised on? How can the less successful aspects of your performance you mentioned be tackled through changes in job content, through training or by other means? Will any changes in the demands made on you in the near future require that some steps be taken now to equip you to deal with them?

## The Appraisal Interview

The agenda for appraisal interview will be based on the headings of the Self-appraisal Form, so the starting point for the whole discussion will be *your* ideas and perceptions (though the appraiser will obviously contribute his or her views too). This means that the major responsibility for making the appraisal interview a successful and effective vehicle for constructive action will be yours. The more thought and preparation you have done for it beforehand, the more you and the company as a whole will get out of it.

# *Appendix B:*

# Appraisal training interview feedback form

*When making your assessment of the appraiser's performance in the practice session, remember to back up your observations with concrete examples. Where you feel there was scope for improvement, GIVE CONSTRUCTIVE SUGGESTIONS AS TO HOW YOU FEEL THE SITUATION MIGHT HAVE BEEN HANDLED BETTER.*

1. How well was the initial period of the appraisal handled (outlining the purpose, and so on)?

Very well  \* – – –\* – – –\* – – –\* – – –\* – – –\* – – –\* – – –\*  Not well
             1    2    3    4    5    6    7

2. To what extent did the interview cover all the areas it was intended to?

Covered all \* – – –\* – – –\* – – –\* – – –\* – – –\* – – –\* – – –\* Poor coverage
          1    2    3    4    5    6    7

3. How successful was the appraiser in encouraging self-assessment by the appraisee?

Successful \* – – –\* – – –\* – – –\* – – –\* – – –\* – – –\* – – –\* Not successful
        1    2    3    4    5    6    7

4. How successful was the appraiser in getting the appraisee involved in solving problems/suggesting ways to improve?

Successful \* – – –\* – – –\* – – –\* – – –\* – – –\* – – –\* – – –\* Not successful
        1    2    3    4    5    6    7

5. How well did the appraiser handle the objective-setting element?

Very well  \* – – –\* – – –\* – – –\* – – –\* – – –\* – – –\* – – –\*  Not well
             1  2    3    4    5    6    7

6. To what extent did the objectives set seem (a) relevant (b) appropriately challenging (c) quantifiable?

Very relevant \*‑ ‑ ‑\*‑ ‑ ‑\*‑ ‑ ‑\*‑ ‑ ‑\*‑ ‑ ‑\*‑ ‑ ‑\*‑ ‑ ‑\* Not relevant
                    1       2       3       4       5       6       7

Appropriately \*‑ ‑ ‑\*‑ ‑ ‑\*‑ ‑ ‑\*‑ ‑ ‑\*‑ ‑ ‑\*‑ ‑ ‑\*‑ ‑ ‑\* Inappropriately
challenging       1       2       3       4       5       6       7    challenging

Quantifiable \*‑ ‑ ‑\*‑ ‑ ‑\*‑ ‑ ‑\*‑ ‑ ‑\*‑ ‑ ‑\*‑ ‑ ‑\*‑ ‑ ‑\* Not
                    1       2       3       4       5       6       7    quantifiable

7. How much attention did the appraiser give to the appraisee's development needs?

Ample       \*‑ ‑ ‑\*‑ ‑ ‑\*‑ ‑ ‑\*‑ ‑ ‑\*‑ ‑ ‑\*‑ ‑ ‑\*‑ ‑ ‑\*  Not
attention     1       2       3       4       5       6       7    enough

8. How well did the appraiser handle any differences in views on the appraisee's performance and achievements?

Very well   \*‑ ‑ ‑\*‑ ‑ ‑\*‑ ‑ ‑\*‑ ‑ ‑\*‑ ‑ ‑\*‑ ‑ ‑\*‑ ‑ ‑\*  Not well
                    1       2       3       4       5       6       7

9. What level of sensitivity did the appraiser display in handling the session?

High        \*‑ ‑ ‑\*‑ ‑ ‑\*‑ ‑ ‑\*‑ ‑ ‑\*‑ ‑ ‑\*‑ ‑ ‑\*‑ ‑ ‑\*  Low
sensitivity   1       2       3       4       5       6       7    sensitivity

10. What sort of balance did the appraiser strike between listening and talking?

Listened    \*‑ ‑ ‑\*‑ ‑ ‑\*‑ ‑ ‑\*‑ ‑ ‑\*‑ ‑ ‑\*‑ ‑ ‑\*‑ ‑ ‑\*  Talked
                    1       2       3       4       5       6       7

# Appendix C(1):

## Example of Appraisal evaluation questionnaires

An example of an evaluation questionnaire sent to *appraisers* (the questionnaire is precoded for computer analysis).

$$\boxed{\ \ |\ \ |\ \ }\quad 1-3$$

### Questionnaire for Appraisers

1. How many staff have you given an appraisal interview to:

$$\boxed{\ \ |\ \ }\quad 4/5$$

Please record your answers to the questions by putting a tick in the appropriate box(es) on the right.

2. Have you yourself every been given an appraisal interview?

Yes $\boxed{\ }$ 1

No $\boxed{\ }$ 2 $\quad$ 6

3. How much time (on average) did you spend in preparing for each of the interviews?

| | | |
|---|---|---|
| Less than ½ hour | $\boxed{\ }$ | 1 |
| ½ hour but less than 1 hour | $\boxed{\ }$ | 2 |
| 1 hour but less than 2 hours | $\boxed{\ }$ | 3 |
| 2 hours or more | $\boxed{\ }$ | 4 |

7 (to the right of rows 2 and 3)

4. When giving the interviews, did you generally find any difficulty in getting the interviewees to:

| | Yes | No | |
|---|---|---|---|
| Agree realistic objectives | | | 8 |
| Comment on their own performance weaknesses | | | 9 |
| Put forward their own solutions to problems | | | 10 |
| | 1 | 2 | |

5. Did you usually find that the interviewee did most of the talking in the interview?

Yes ☐ 1
No ☐ 2    11

6. Do you feel that the appraisees were being frank with you in the interview?

Yes, all of them ☐ 1
Yes, most of them ☐ 2
Yes, some of them ☐ 3    12
None of them ☐ 4

7. Did any of the appraisals you conducted make you aware of any staff problems or job problems (e.g. lack of clear job definition, too heavy or too light a workload) that you had not previously known about?

| | Yes | No | |
|---|---|---|---|
| Made me aware of job problems | | | 13 |
| Made me aware of staff problems | | | 14 |
| | 1 | 2 | |

8. Did anything you learned in the appraisal cause you to modify your assessment of the interviewee?

Yes, in one or more cases ☐ 1

Never ☐ 2

15

9. Do you think that the appraisals have, either directly or indirectly, led to any improvement in the job performance of the interviewees?

Yes, in every case ☐ 1

Yes, in some cases ☐ 2

No ☐ 3

Too soon to tell ☐ 4

16

10. Generally speaking, do you think you got anything useful out of the appraisals you gave?

Yes ☐ 1

No ☐ 2

17

11. Do you feel that the appraisal scheme fits in with your normal style of management?

Yes ☐ 1

No ☐ 2

18

12. How do you, as a manager, feel about the performance appraisal scheme?

I am greatly in favour of it ☐ 1

I am in favour of it ☐ 2

I am indifferent to it ☐ 3 19

I am against it ☐ 4

I am strongly against it ☐ 5

13. Do you feel you have had adequate training and preparation to carry out the appraisals?

Yes ☐ 1
No ☐ 2   20

Thank you for your cooperation: please add any comments you would like to make on the back of the Questionnaire.

## Appendix C(2):

# Example of appraisal evaluation questionnaires

An example of an evaluation questionnaire sent to *appraisees* (again the questionnaire is pre-coded for computer analysis). The questionnaires were given numerical codes before being sent out, so that the biographical data on each potential respondent was known.

**CONFIDENTIAL**

☐☐☐☐☐☐  1 – 6

1.  How many times have you been given an appraisal interview?

    Once ☐ 1
    Twice ☐ 2  7
    Three times or more ☐ 3

    (If you have been given more than one, please relate your answers to the most recent one.)

2.  How long is it since you last had an appraisal?

    Less than 1 month ☐ 1
    1 month but less than 3 months ☐ 2
    3 months but less than 6 months ☐ 3  8
    6 months or more ☐ 4

3.  How much advance warning were you given that you were going to be interviewed?

    No advance warning ☐ 1
    Less than 1 day ☐ 2
    1 day but less than 3 days ☐ 3  9
    3 days or more ☐ 4

4.  How long did the interview last?

|                    |     |      |
| ------------------ | --- | ---- |
| Less than ½ hour   |     | 1    |
| ½ – 1 hour         |     | 2 10 |
| Over 1 hour        |     | 3    |

5.  Did the interviewer mention any parts of the job you had done particularly well?

|     |     |      |
| --- | --- | ---- |
| Yes |     | 1    |
| No  |     | 2    | 11

6.  Was there any mention or dicussion of the weaker aspects of your performance in the job during the interview?

|     |     |      |
| --- | --- | ---- |
| Yes |     | 1    |
| No  |     | 2    | 12

7.  Do you feel that the interviewer had a reasonably fair idea of your performance in the job?

|     |     |      |
| --- | --- | ---- |
| Yes |     | 1    |
| No  |     | 2    | 13

8.  What impression did you get of how the interviewer considered your performance in the job? That he/she thought it was:

|                           |     |      |
| ------------------------- | --- | ---- |
| Outstanding               |     | 1    |
| Very Good                 |     | 2    |
| Good                      |     | 3    |
| Fair                      |     | 4 14 |
| Not quite adequate        |     | 5    |
| Unsatisfactory            |     | 6    |
| (Got no impression at all)|     | 7    |

9 . Were your training needs mentioned or discussed in the interview?

Yes ☐ 1

No ☐ 2

15

10. Did you get the impression that the interviewer was being completely frank with you in the interview?

Yes ☐ 1

No ☐ 2

16

11. To what extent did the interviewer agree with your own assessment of your performance?

To a large extent ☐ 1

To some extent ☐ 2

Not very much ☐ 3 17

Not at all ☐ 4

Difficult to say ☐ 5

12. Were you able to agree with the interviewer on what your objectives should be for next year?

Yes ☐ 1

No ☐ 2

18

13. Do you feel these objectives are reasonable?

Yes ☐ 1

No ☐ 2

19

14. Did any firm proposals for action (e.g. changing your work methods, giving you more responsibility or guidance, recommending a transfer, etc.) come out of the appraisal?

Yes ☐ 1

No ☐ 2

20

15. Did the interview make you feel that you *wanted* to improve your performance in the job?

| | | |
|---|---|---|
| Yes | ☐ | 1 |
| No | ☐ | 2 21 |
| I did not get the impression that there was any real need to | ☐ | 3 |

16. After the appraisal, were you any clearer in your own mind about what you could do to improve your work?

| | | |
|---|---|---|
| Yes | ☐ | 1 |
| No | ☐ | 2 |

22

17. Do you think the appraisal interview has led to, or is likely to lead to, any improvement in your job performance?

| | | |
|---|---|---|
| Yes, a considerable improvement | ☐ | 1 |
| Yes, a slight improvement | ☐ | 2 |
| Neither improvement nor deterioration | ☐ | 3 23 |
| No, a slight deterioration | ☐ | 4 |
| No, a considerable deterioration | ☐ | 5 |

18. Has the fact that you have had an appraisal interview affected your general satisfaction with the job?

| | | |
|---|---|---|
| It has greatly increased my satisfaction | ☐ | 1 |
| It has slightly increased my satisfaction | ☐ | 2 |
| It has not affected my satisfaction | ☐ | 3 24 |
| It has slightly decreased my satisfaction | ☐ | 4 |
| It has greatly decreased my satisfaction | ☐ | 5 |

19. How do you feel about performance appraisals?

| | |
|---|---|
| I am strongly in favour of them | ☐ 1 |
| I am slightly in favour of them | ☐ 2 |
| I am neither for nor against them | ☐ 3 25 |
| I am slightly against them | ☐ 4 |
| I am strongly against them | ☐ 5 |

20. Below are a number of statements describing various features of appraisal interviews. They are arranged in pairs, the two statements in each pair being in contrast to one another. The line which joins the two statements in each pair is divided into six sections. Please examine each statement in a pair and then decide which comes closest to describing the interview which you had; the better it describes your interview, the nearer that end of the line you should put your tick. (Ignore the boxes at the side of these statements.)

*EXAMPLE:* Please put your tick through the line like this

| The interviewer was friendly | ⊢─✓─┼─┼─┼─┤ | The interviewer was hostile |
|---|---|---|

---

| The interviewer did nearly all the talking in the interview | ⊢─┼─┼─┼─┼─┤ | I did most of the talking in the interview | ☐ 26 |
|---|---|---|---|
| The interviewer seemed wholly concerned with *assessing* my work performance over the last year | ⊢─┼─┼─┼─┼─┤ | The interviewer seemed chiefly interested in *improving* my work performance in the year ahead | ☐ 27 |

| | | |
|---|---|---|
| I felt it would have been best not to pursue the matter where points of disagreement arose | ├─┼─┼─┼─┼─┤ | The interviewer made me feel that I was free to discuss points of disagreement 28 |
| The interviewer did not allow me to offer my viewpoint on the way I coped with the job | ├─┼─┼─┼─┼─┤ | The interviewer allowed me to put forward my own views on how I had coped with the job 29 |
| The interviewer seemed to have to have made up his/her mind about things before the interview started | ├─┼─┼─┼─┼─┤ | I got the impression that the interviewer was willing to take a new view on things in the light of what I said 30 |
| Almost all the ideas for getting round job difficulties came from the interviewer | ├─┼─┼─┼─┼─┤ | I provided most of the solutions to the problems we discussed 31 |
| The interviewer made no attempt to understand my feelings about the job | ├─┼─┼─┼─┼─┤ | The interviewer made every attempt to understand the way I felt about the job 32 |
| The interviewer did not appear to be paying attention when I was speaking | ├─┼─┼─┼─┼─┤ | The interviewer listened most attentively whenever I spoke 33 |

| The interviewer did not invite me to put forward any ideas or suggestions about the job | ⊢―+―+―+―⊣ | The interviewer continually pressed me for *my* ideas and suggestions about the job | [ ] 34 |

| The interviewer did not try to help me clarify my own thoughts about the job | ⊢―+―+―+―⊣ | The interviewer tried to help me clarify my own thoughts about the job | [ ] 35 |

Please use the back of the questionnaire if you have any comments on, or suggestions for changes in, the appraisal scheme, or if there are any points arising out of this questionnaire which you wish to say more about.

Please check through to see that nothing has been left out. Many thanks for your help and cooperation.

# Appendix D:

## Attitude measures

There are a number of questionnaire measures that are both relevant to assessing broad employee attitudes and motivation, and are readily available. These include:

- The Organisational Commitment Scale produced by Cook and Wall (1980). This breaks down into three components: organisational loyalty, organisational identification and organisational involvement.
- The Job Satisfaction Scale (Warr, Cook and Wall, 1979). This taps satisfaction with 15 different aspects of work, broadly grouped into intrinsic and extrinsic job satisfaction.

Both of the above, and several others (covering factors such as goal clarity), were used in Part 2 of the IPM report on performance management, and the reader can find the questionnaire items and various other details given there by Fletcher and Williams (IPM, 1992). The report data, about a number of private and public sector organisations, should facilitate making comparisons for other companies using the scales. There are, however, other measures, such as:

- Job Involvement (Lodahl and Kejner, 1965). This measures the extent to which a person identifies psychologically with work and the importance of work in their self image.
- Another measure of Organisational Commitment, provided by Mowday, Steers and Porter (1979), consisting of 15 items.

## *Appendix E:*

# An example of an external assessment report

This example (the candidate details are, of course, fictitious) is based on an assessment procedure where the candidate had been referred for individual external assessment as part of a wider development activity within one division of a major UK company. All senior managers within the division were assessed, and the results fed back to them by the assessor. At a later date, the assessment report was discussed with each of them by a management development manager, who looked at the findings in the context of career planning within the company. The assessment data were also used to review the structure and team-work within the division. All those who went through the assessment process did so voluntarily – in fact, they were keen to do so.

The report is based primarily on psychometric tests, including two personality measures and four cognitive ability tests. The procedure also included an interview of around two hours. All test scores are quoted in relation to specific senior management norms. This is, of course, only one example of how such reports can be presented and structured; there are many variations, some of which suit particular needs better than others.

# PERSONAL IN CONFIDENCE

## EXTERNAL ASSESSMENT REPORT

**[Specimen Copy Only]**

**Name** ALAN SMITH

**Date** 18 January 1992

**Assessor** Dr Clive Fletcher

This report is primarily concerned with judgments about how the candidate will behave at work. It is less concerned with the reasons why he or she will behave in any particular way; nor does it comment on technical or professional competence. The information given here must be treated as strictly confidential and should only be made available to staff who have responsibility for employment or career planning decisions relating to this individual. The report should not be used if more than five years have elapsed since it was written.

**Name**: Alan Smith

**Date of Birth**: 28 June 1946

**Age**: 45

## EDUCATIONAL/PROFESSIONAL QUALIFICATIONS

1964 – 68 Leicester University
BSc Hons (2:2) Chemistry

1968 – 69 Salford University
MBA

## CAREER HISTORY

| | | |
|---|---|---|
| 1969 – 71 | XYZ Industries | Market Research post |
| 1971 – 74 | Jones Electrical Ltd | Various posts in Corporate and Financial Planning |
| 1974 – 86 | LFC Engineering Ltd | Marketing Planning Manager |
| | | Major Accounts Marketing Manager |
| | | Marketing Planning Manager (Overseas) |
| | | Marketing Manager, Ireland |
| | | Manager, Sales Force Development (79/81) |
| | | Marketing Manager, Systems (81/83) |
| | | Regional Systems Marketing Manager (83/85) |
| | | Business Manager, G Division (85/86) |
| 1986 – | Anyco plc | Head of Overseas Coordination Unit (86/88) |
| | | GM Marketing Planning (88/90) |
| | | Manager, Programmes and Quality (1990 – ) |

**Intellectual Effectiveness**

Synopsis

Mr Smith has a good level of intellectual effectiveness. Compared to senior managers as a group, he is below average on logical thinking ability, average on verbal ability, above average on imaginative thinking ability and outstanding on numerical ability.

Numerical ability

His score on the test of his ability to make correct decisions and inferences from numerical and statistical data was outstanding, and puts him in the top 10% of senior managers. He worked very quickly and completed the test, attaining a reasonable level of accuracy.

Verbal ability

He scored at the lower end of the average range on the test of vocabulary and verbal reasoning. In conversation, he expresses himself carefully and thoughtfully.

Logical thinking

His performance on the test of critical thinking, covering the dispassionate analysis of information, arguments, inferences and deductions, was below average and places him in the bottom 20% of senior managers. He started well on the test, his performance trailing off at the end. His analytical ability may not be all that strong.

Imaginative thinking

The test of the quantity and quality of his ideas showed him to be outstanding on the former and above average on the latter. He had many ideas, though some of them were fairly routine and simply involved variations on a theme. However, he did display a capacity for some more imaginative and original insights in his thinking about new situations.

## Work Approach

### General approach

Mr Smith prefers to take a very slow, deliberate, highly structured and cautious approach to his work. He will plan ahead and will emphasise quality and long-term perspectives in what he does. His style is far from dynamic; he is better at thinking than at doing, and at organising rather than delivering.

### Productivity

Compared to most senior managers, he is very low on drive. He will tend to work at his own steady pace, and he will tire more quickly than most. He will, however, usually be well organised. Overall, though, productivity is unlikely to be his strong point.

### Quality of work

He is deeply thoughtful and will seldom be content to take things at face value. He will want to reflect on issues in some depth, asking questions and discussing the various implications of different lines of action. He will be very aware of the strategic picture, and will plan ahead in considerable detail. In most cases, this will lead to high quality of output. However, there will be times when he finds it hard to resolve the complexity of the issues, and in the pursuit of perfectionist standards loses sight of the more immediate concerns.

### Mastery of detail

He will be extremely attentive to detail and will exercise great care in handling them, tending to spend too long on them. He will delegate reasonably willingly, though he will expect his subordinates to be just as precise as he himself is.

## Decision-making

He will seek to avoid risks at all costs, and will be very unadventurous and cautious in his attitude to decisions. He will want a lot of time to think things through, which may not always actually improve the final analysis anyway. His judgement will be slow in forming, but it will usually be reliable if overly-conservative.

## Tolerance for pressure

Mr Smith is a little more emotional than the average, but he is extremely restrained and controlled in the way he expresses his feelings: indeed, he will seldom let them show through at all. Very occasionally, he can let his frustrations affect his judgment and make a snap decision on emotional rather than logical grounds. He will react slowly to pressure, stepping back to give himself time to analyse the situation and organise his tactics for dealing with it. Both his lack of drive and his normal style of working make him unsuited to high pressure, though a degree of moderate pressure will facilitate his performance by ensuring that he does not take too long over things.

## Flexibility

Whilst he has a positive attitude to the idea of change, he will only really be happy in dealing with it when he can do so in a clearly planned and well-organised manner. He will be rather slow, rigid and uncomfortable when faced with rapid changes that produce uncertainty and ambiguity, and where he cannot take the time out to review the situation in some depth.

## Ambition

He is not as ambitious in the conventional sense as he was a few years ago; his values have changed and he is more centred on personal satisfactions arising from family relationships and from developing others. He is also less interested in, and satisfied by, his present role. He is motivated mainly by intellectual interests and the desire to be allowed to work to the high standards he sets for himself.

## Relationships With Others

### General impact

Mr Smith is an extremely polite, courteous man who tries to act in accordance with his strong beliefs about the way people should be treated. He is friendly and rather shy, and while he makes a favourable impression on first meeting, his impact on colleagues in the longer term will suffer from his great reluctance to assert himself.

### Relationships with superiors

Superiors will find that he wants them to be consistent – he will feel unhappy with rapid changes of direction or arrangements. He will need to know where he stands, and he will appreciate a boss who gives him plenty of time to discuss ideas and strategy. It will not be important to him to get to know his boss on close personal terms – he will not mind some distance in that sense as long as he feels on the same wavelength. Those above him will find that he responds best to sensitive and courteous handling, and that he seldom expresses himself forcefully. They will find that he is too cautious to display much initiative, and that he needs gentle pressure to keep him moving things forward at a reasonable pace. He will be a conscientious but fairly low-profile subordinate who does not make any attempt to project himself to get credit from his superiors.

### Relationships with peers

He is not very outgoing and will keep socialising to a minimum. Peers will find him to be amiable and always well-mannered in his conduct towards them. He will take this a little too far in some respects, not pressing home his ideas firmly enough and allowing himself to be talked-over rather too easily. He will tend to offer his views and suggestions and leave it to others to decide whether they want to adopt them, instead of actively seeking to persuade and influence his colleagues. They will probably feel that he is altogether too cautious and that he holds them back, while he for his part will see them as too quick to adopt the easy or the short-term solution. However, he will be a cooperative and supportive member of the team who does not seek to be at the centre of attention or to boost his own personal standing at the expense of others. He will seldom take the leadership role unless asked.

### Relationship with subordinates

Subordinates will find that he places emphasis on team development and on trying to balance their contributions in the most effective way. He will spend time and effort in coaching and supporting his staff, and he will ensure that they get credit for their achievements even at some cost to his own standing. Subordinates will find that he delegates willingly and that he exerts only light control. He will, however, plan their work in some detail at the outset, and he will expect high standards. But he will not drive them hard, and he will be reluctant to take a firm line with poor performers.

## Summary and Integration

Mr Smith has a good level of intellectual ability, with particular strength in his capacity for numerical reasoning. He is something of a perfectionist, though he might not see it entirely that way himself. A deeply thoughtful man, he abhors the superficial and short-term solutions, and continually looks beyond the immediate situation to more strategic considerations. He will plan ahead in detail, adopting a highly structured approach that puts the emphasis on attaining quality output, avoiding errors and risks, and attending to details. Not surprisingly, this style of working is not well suited to sustained high pressure, and he will prefer to operate at a much more deliberate and steady pace. Compared to senior managers as a group, he is very low on drive and will tend to progress tasks fairly slowly, perhaps becoming tired rather more quickly than some of his contemporaries. Productivity, in terms of sheer speed and volume, is unlikely to be his strong point. He has a positive attitude to change, at least intellectually, but he will want to deal with it in a planned and organised way; he will be much less sure and confident in his handling of situations where there is a degree of uncertainty and ambiguity. He will be cautious in his decision-making, wanting time to think things through. He is a little more emotional than the average, though he is very restrained and controlled and will seldom let his feelings show. He is no longer very ambitious in the sense of wanting to climb to the top of an organisation.

Colleagues will find that Mr Smith is a friendly, though somewhat shy, man who places great store by respect and courtesy − both in the way he treats others and in the way they treat him. Perhaps this is the cause, or the effect, of his reluctance to assert himself at all forcefully. He will be patient and restrained in his conduct, and will tend to adopt a low profile. He will avoid confrontation and will seldom take the leadership role unless asked. Colleagues at all levels will find that he does not seek to take personal credit, and that he is unselfish and supportive in his contribution to the team effort. There will be times when he is perhaps undervalued as a result, and when he does not exert as much influence as he should. Superiors will find that he needs consistency of direction on their part and to know where he stands with them. He will want the opportunity to discuss ideas and strategy with his boss, though he will not be concerned about developing a more personal relationship with him. His superiors will probably feel that he is too cautious to show much initiative, and his peers will similarly see him as too careful and lacking in adventure − though they will appreciate his cooperative attitude. He will put time and effort into developing his own subordinates and he will make sure they get full credit for their achievements. He will delegate willingly within the thoroughly-planned framework he provides for his staff to work to. He will not push his subordinates very hard.

# General Evaluation of Alan Smith for ANYCO PLC

Main assets

- Generally good intellectual ability; outstanding in capacity for numerical reasoning
- Thoughtful, careful, quality-oriented approach
- Attentive to details and avoids errors
- Emotionally well controlled and restrained
- Plans ahead in detail; a strategic thinker
- Friendly, courteous individual; makes a good first impression
- Cooperative, supportive and unselfish team man
- Puts time and effort into developing subordinates
- Delegates sensibly

Main limitations

- Can be excessively cautious and may miss opportunities
- Perfectionist standards likely to be at some cost to speed and flexibility of response
- Very low on drive; adverse effects on productivity and tolerance of pressure
- Extremely reluctant to assert himself forcefully; probably lacks influence as a result
- Could push subordinates harder and be more willing to take a firm line at times

## Development Needs

Mr Smith has good intellectual ability and will no doubt make a substantial contribution to the organisation in the right role. Finding that role is particularly important in his case, as he will not be all that versatile or adaptable. He clearly does not feel entirely happy in his present job. He feels he is going round in small circles, and misses the international marketing scene to some extent. More than that, though, he sees himself as a thinker and planner more than a doer and implementer, and probably feels he is not used to his best ability in his job.

The kind of position that he will perform best in is one where he can take time to think things through without being allowed to dwell on them excessively. He will be at his best in roles that call for long-term planning and strategy, attention to detail, avoidance of risks, numerical reasoning power, cooperation and team work, and a supportive management style with subordinates. He will be least effective where the need is for tolerance of high pressure, for the ability to cope with uncertainty and ambiguity, for quick and flexible responses, for a dynamic and energetic style, for assertiveness and the ability to handle conflict, and for risk-taking.

Mr Smith has enjoyed and derived great satisfaction from those times when he has been placed in a training or staff development position, and it may well be that he will increasingly find himself drawn in that direction, which would probably play to his strengths. He likes the world of ideas, and he has values that suit him to more teaching and research type roles.

For the future, he needs to understand that his approach is perhaps more extreme than he realises, and that while it produces real advantages in some directions, it inevitably has its limitations. He needs to be a little more flexible and dynamic, and to learn to take more risks – not least in asserting himself with greater determination. Training may help in respect of this last quality, though it seems to be sufficiently ingrained to make it quite difficult to change.

# Index